MW01093609

JESUS
THE Harmony

Jesus
THE Harmony

Gospel Sonnets
for 366 Days

Gracia M. Grindal

Fortress Press

Minneapolis

JESUS THE HARMONY
Gospel Sonnets for 366 Days

Print ISBN: 978-1-5064-6455-8
eBook ISBN: 978-1-5064-6456-5

Cover Design: Marti Naughton
Cover Images: "I Am the Resurrection" (John 11:17–44) by
Mike Moyers. Used by permission.

To the Bible study group at the
Norwegian Lutheran Memorial Church,
which has supported me in prayer and
conversation over the past years
and especially during this project

contents

The Poet's Birthing Bed

ix

Introduction: The Harmony

xi

The Sonnets

xvii

Part One
The Life of Jesus before His Public Ministry

1

Part Two
The Public Ministry of Jesus

31

THE POET'S BIRTHING BED

Toward evening, when the poet slows
To seek her benediction,
She knows where there awaits repose,
But more—an expectation.
It's to her sonnet birthing bed
Where she will be not quite alone;
The Three, the Father at its head
And at its foot, the Son enthroned.
And softly as mid rustling leaves
In songful sighs and tuneful tongue
The whispering Spirit gently breathes
The longed-for lines, all fresh and young.

I write and dedicate this poem to poet Gracia Grindal, who has engaged in this daunting project of writing 366 sonnets on the life of Jesus using all four Gospels. Her modus operandi has been fascinating. Daytimes she mulled over that day's portion, and at bedtime, with laptop ready, she wrote the new sonnet. In a relatively short time, she put it to bed. The results are inspiring.

Paul Estrem Ofstedal (+), 2019

Introduction:
The Harmony

Modern readers of these sonnets may wonder what *The Harmony of the Gospels* is and why it was used as the list of texts on which these sonnets meditate. Harmonies, which go back to the second century after our Lord, tell the life of Jesus using all four Gospels, combining them into a single narrative. While each of the four Gospels tells the story of Jesus and they are, for the most part, alike, there are differences in chronology and emphases. A harmony attempted to tell the story as one book, facing the differences but explaining them. It was first intended as a devotional aid for people who wanted to read the life of Jesus in one document. Over the centuries, it remained a devotional guide to the life of Jesus, without supplanting the four Gospels—Matthew, Mark, Luke, and John.

The first harmonizer was Tatian (120–73), the Syrian scholar of the second century whose harmony *Diatesseron* (meaning in Greek "through four" or "out of four" of the Gospels) of 150 CE was widely used by the Syrian church until the fifth century. The name suggests that Tatian was well aware of the four Gospels and assumed they were already part of the canon of the New

Testament. Although he was later declared a heretic, his work remained popular among Syrian Christians and spread to others in the early church. The attempt would not be the last.

A number of early church scholars tried their hand at a harmony. Augustine, the great theologian of the early church, wrote *The Harmony of the Gospels* (*De consensu evangeliorum*), treating the issues that a harmony presented in both chronology and emphases. In the attempt to harmonize the four Gospels and explain the reasons for the various differences in them, the scholars engaged in serious biblical exegesis that continues to prove edifying.

The Middle Ages produced a few harmonies—one in Middle Dutch and one in Middle English, known as the *Pepsyian*. In any event, these efforts indicate an interest in the project over the millennia.

The period of the Reformation produced more harmonies. John Calvin and others in the Reformed movement worked on ones. The Lutheran theologian Martin Chemnitz (1522–86) began a harmony that was continued by Polycarp Leyser (1552–1633) and finished by John Gerhard (1582–1637), *The Harmony of the Four Evangelists*.[1] They have been translated and published

---

[1] This harmony appears in multiple volumes, translated by Richard J. Dinda, copyright © 2000, and published by The Center for the Study of Lutheran Orthodoxy, Malone, TX (2009–2014). This translation is based on the edition with the title *The Harmony of the Four Evangelists which the very renowned Theologian, Martin Chemnitz, began very auspiciously: which Dr. Polycarp Leyser continued and which Dr. John Gerhard Completed most Fruitfully, Both of Who were Theologians of No Less Renown*, published 1703 in Hamburg, Germany.

and are thick books filled with closely argued and edifying biblical scholarship and thought, and they are still well worth reading.

In the first half of the nineteenth century, the issue of the lack of harmony among the four Gospels became troubling to many. As scholars started writing their versions of the life of Jesus, they stressed the incompatibilities of the four Gospels, and some used them to assert that the Gospels were nothing but myths deluding people into believing in Jesus. David Friedrich Strauss's (1808–74) *The Life of Jesus Critically Examined* (*Das Leben Jesu kritisch bearbeitet*, 1835–36) was the first. His work helped destroy the faith of many a believer, including that of the English author George Eliot (1819–80), who translated Strauss into English. It began the movement known as the quest for the historical Jesus with the historical-critical method of reading Scripture.

Modern Bible scholars using historical-critical methods to look at the material behind the texts were not always searching to edify readers of Scripture. Their work often had the intention or at least the effect of corroding faith. The method often made preaching difficult, leaving exegetes with fragments, not whole passages. It distanced the reader from Scripture, focusing on the editor or writer rather than the Savior.

Contemporary liturgical churches know a part of the harmony of Jesus' life very well: the reading of Christ's passion on Palm Sunday / Passion Sunday, which combines all of the salient texts in the four Gospels necessary to tell the story. It is very much with us as a tradition that many congregations observe on Passion Sunday. The Seven Last Words from the Cross come from a harmonization of the Gospels. Without a harmony, we would not have had such a fruitful topic upon which to meditate. The passion readings were printed in hymnals of the past so people could read a harmonized account of Jesus' passion and be edified by it during Lent.

The great hymn writer of Iceland Hallgrímur Pétursson (1614–74) wrote a series of fifty hymn meditations for Lent, using harmony texts as his source. These hymns are still at the center of Icelandic piety, as they are read in homes, in churches, and on national radio every day during Lent. The passion history inspired many other hymn writers to write hymns using a harmony as their inspiration. In some regards, one could think of harmonies as the oldest devotional aids in the church.

One of the more surprising efforts to use a harmony is the extensive number of paintings, some 350, done by the French painter Jacques Joseph Tissot (1836–1902). He had been a popular genre painter of Parisian fashion, but after a conversion experience in 1886, he went to the Holy Land to research the life of Jesus and paint scenes from it using harmony texts. Most of that collection is now in the Brooklyn Museum. The paintings regularly appear in resources that use art to illustrate or comment on the various biblical lessons in the numerous lectionaries being used today.

Harmonies continue to be a rich source for devotion. One can go online and find several suggested lists of biblical passages to be treated in a harmony. They are all fairly similar, although the order may vary depending on which Gospel is used as the main source—some prefer Luke to Matthew, but others use Matthew as their starting point. My source for the passages was *The Gospel: Synopsis, Harmony, Explanatory Notes*, a book by Johannes Thorbjørnson Ylvisaker (1845–1917), the English translation of which was published posthumously by Augsburg Publishing House in 1918.

The late pastor Paul Ofstedal gave me a copy of this book to use—it had been a gift from his father, Rudy Ofstedal, to him in 1950. It is a thick book—almost eight hundred pages—of thoughtful and illuminating commentary. Ylvisaker, a longtime professor of New Testament at Luther Seminary from 1876 to 1917, studied at Leipzig and Oslo in the 1880s, where he grappled with the historical criticism of the Bible. After years of teaching the New Testament, especially the four Gospels, he decided to wade into this territory, partly because of what he regarded as a need to answer these critics of Scripture who had, as he wrote, "trampled the holy underfoot."[2]

A learned man, he read the works of all the "cultured despisers" of the faith in his time and answered them trenchantly. Most interesting are his rich reflections on the Scripture itself. There is always something surprising in his expositions of the texts, from which I learned much. The order I have used for the sonnets is the order as they appear in Ylvisaker's book.

---

[2] Johannes Thorbjørnson Ylvisaker, *The Gospel: Synopsis, Harmony, Explanatory Notes* (Minneapolis: Augsburg, 1918), 10.

THE sonnets

Because these sonnets deal discretely with one passage at a time, I do not have to solve the issues posed by a harmony, but I have benefited from the various exegetical works of those compiling such harmonies. And I have used the texts in the order that most harmonies use for the life of Christ. These will not be the order of any one of the Gospels but will be the way scholars have harmonized them into a coherent narrative built on all four Gospels.

These sonnets are not prayers and are not often personal; rather, they are reflections on the Gospel passages in Johannes Thorbjørnson Ylvisaker's harmony. They are more like brief sermons or homilies. They should enrich one's meditations on the biblical passage and enhance one's sense of Jesus in the biblical story as they tell the red thread of salvation. The second reading listed is the one most closely connected to the Gospel passage, and the third is less so. In choosing those auxiliary lessons, I have included every book in the Bible. I was struck during this part of the work by the frequency with which Jesus refers to Leviticus and Deuteronomy, Daniel, Psalms, and Proverbs. The Gospel writers cannot imagine Jesus without the Old Testament; it is the way they see Jesus and tell his story. I learned much about the Old Testament in doing this work as well, something that I hope the readers will see and be helped by. Prayer before or after reading the biblical passage and the sonnet is the way that I would imagine will enable the most fruitful reading of the sonnets.

The sonnets are printed with the title of the work, an event or teaching in Jesus' life. They will be easily recognizable from the Scripture lesson recommended at the bottom of the sonnet. For ease of reference, a number is assigned to each sonnet, one for every day, including a leap year. The first sonnet, an "Invocation," is an introduction to the entire work and is not counted in the series. Since there are only 160 Scripture lessons referenced in the Ylvisasker harmony, I have frequently written several sonnets on one text. Again, the title of the sonnet and the key texts at the bottom of the sonnet will provide the context of each reading.

Ylvisaker was not my only companion in this work. Many recent books on Jesus are, in effect, harmonies, since they attempt to tell the whole story of Jesus in a chronological form. Jaroslav Pelikan's *Jesus through the Centuries: His Place in Culture* (Yale University Press, 1999) was my first foray into the topic, long before this work, but one I returned to during this project. Fredrick Dale Bruner's two-volume work, *Matthew: A Commentary* (vols. 1 and 2, expanded editions, Eerdmans, 2007), and *The Gospel of John: A Commentary* (Eerdmans, 2012) helped my thinking immensely, and close readers may note his influence in my work, especially in sonnet 174 on the temple tax and Peter finding a coin in the fish to pay it. Because Bruner always included comments from the tradition and the great forerunners, such as Chrysostom, Augustine, Luther, and Calvin, he gave me a broader sense for the tradition's concerns, all the way back to Irenaeus.

I frequently turned to other major sources—among them, Pope Benedict's *Jesus of Nazareth* (Ignatius Press, 2008). It was helpful, alongside N. T. Wright's *Simply Jesus: A New Vision of Who He Was, What He Did, and Why He Matters* (HarperOne, reprint 2018); Timothy Keller's book on Mark, *Jesus the King* (Penguin, 2013); David Tiede's *Luke: Augsburg Commentary on the New Testament* (Augsburg Publishing House, 1988); and Luke Timothy Johnson's lectures in the Great Courses series of the Teaching Company, *Jesus and the Gospels* (2004). All were instructive and helpful.

While I was no doubter when I began, about midway, in the summer, the fact that Jesus was God incarnate began to overwhelm me. Three main images seemed most pervasive to me: Jesus and the faith as a seed, Jesus as the temple, and Jesus as king of a reality we can only catch glimpses of now and then but who is very much present in our daily lives. These images deepened as I wrote. The idea that the imagery for heaven was obsolete began to strike me as being less and less helpful. Even if they are images of a world that we no longer believe in, they still speak concretely to readers. The idea that they did not exist because we could not see them seemed even stranger than it did in my freshman Bible class. The only way we can speak of realities that we cannot sense is through imagery that may even cause us a kind of rapture with their beauty. Heaven and eternity became ways to speak of that which we cannot know with our senses but believe in. The King James Bible Version translates Hebrews 11:1 in the following way: "Now faith is the substance of things hoped for, the evidence of things unseen." This richly rhetorical sentence with echoes of Greek rhetoric has always fascinated me with its nice balance even as it eluded me. What is a substance hoped for? Or evidence of the unseen? I now have a better grasp of the phrase. As Paul says in his great love chapter, 1 Corinthians 13:9–10, one day we will see in full, no longer in part. Maybe it will be like being healed of blindness as Christ unveils the new world promised to us in his death and resurrection.

This year of writing has helped me grasp that mystery more clearly, but it is still a mystery. The project became a holy obsession each night as I took up the work and meditated on one more passage in the life of Jesus. Sometimes the more I worried during the day that the passage did not have enough to write about, the more surprised I would be by what came to me as I tried to fit the work into the sonnet form.

The form of an English sonnet—with its fourteen lines of iambic pentameter (usually from nine to fourteen syllables a line with five beats per line), a turn at about line eight, a closing couplet, and rhymes—always led me into a surprise, which I hope is evident in the sonnets. To many, form is something of a straitjacket that allows for no personal expression. That is the popularly held opinion today, but when one is searching for a rhyme or trying to fit an idea into a meter, one's unconscious mind is busily at work bringing up ideas that mere thought would not have found. And are almost always surprising.

These sonnets are more like a string of pearls than a single edifice. Although together they may amount to something, each should be contemplated on its own alongside the Scripture lessons. There is a gathering narrative pulse pressing toward the end of the work. Reading them all at once, however, will be too much. While a harmony does not fit with the liturgical calendar, it can be easily used to augment one's concentration on the church year. The first twenty-four sonnets treat the Advent–Christmas stories and can fit into that time. There are fifty sonnets on the life of Christ from Holy Thursday to Easter morning that follow the entire season of Lent nicely. I used the work of Hallgrímur Pétursson to choose those texts, since he made use of the traditional passion harmony common among Lutherans.

Since there are about 160 passages in most harmonies, I expanded the treatment of some of the great parables, events, teachings, and so on. The Lenten sonnets expand on the topics as per the traditional harmony of the Passion Sunday readings. The parable of the prodigal son and the events in the raising of Lazarus seemed to be well worth more sonnets than one. For example, the Sermon on the Mount with the Lord's Prayer in Matthew 5–7, the bread of life discourses in John 6–7, and the farewell discourses of Jesus in John 13–17 also became rich topics on which to meditate with more than one sonnet.

As I close out this rather intense year of writing, I am left in wonder. And a bit of disappointment. Every topic could have been more perfectly explored in several more, if not an infinite number of, treatments. No one can exhaust the topic of our Lord Jesus in a lifetime, let alone a year. God's word keeps surprising and is new every morning. The sonnets could all be added to or rewritten or reworked many times again. One could write such a sonnet every day for the rest of one's life and never run out of new things to say. That is the miracle of Scripture and of Jesus. The Christian life is always surprising.

This work would not have been possible without a conversation with my colleague Walter Sundberg as to how to treat the sonnets on the story of Jesus, which I had begun to write in a rather dilatory way. They needed a theme. He came up with the idea of using a harmony. It was a wonderful thing, and it has been my focus over the past year. That Scott Tunseth, editor at Fortress Press, saw the possibilities of the works when he saw the first part is also reason for gratitude.

Friends and colleagues have been supportive and helpful. Some have read many of the sonnets. Before his death, my good friend Paul Ofstedal read through more than half of the sonnets and made helpful comments and editorial suggestions, and for that, I am grateful. The bishop emeritus of Iceland, Karl Sigurbjörnsson, has also been extremely supportive. Himself a poet, hymn writer, theologian, preacher, and great raconteur of things Icelandic, he has been a stalwart supporter through this work, as has my friend in Denmark, pastor Lisbeth Smedegaard Andersen, who is also a theologian, hymn writer, and poet. Pastor Norm Olsen of Cyrus, Minnesota, an old colleague and friend, read them at the end. I am so grateful for all these helps.

INVOCATION

Sing, Holy Spirit, sing and teach my pen
To write the harmony of Jesus Christ,
Showing in miniatures how God loved men
And women ready to make his sacrifice,
To save us from Eve's curious reaching out
Into the sweet delusions of the fall.
Make each sonnet gleam with faith, not doubt,
Shining like a lustrous pearl that daily calls
Readers to meditate on its milky gem,
Which hides and points to beauties of large degrees,
Like the gates of pearl in the new Jerusalem
Drawing us forward to the glassy seas
Where Christ has made a place for us to dwell
With beauties beyond what words can ever tell.

Revelation 21:15–21; John 14:1–4

Part One

THE Life of Jesus before His public ministry

1

THE PREEXISTENCE OF CHRIST

The sound of light breaking into time,
Wave on wave, giving the spirit flesh,
A new dimension, making the cosmos rhyme.
He spoke the galaxies and gave dust breath
Out of eternity, bringing us light;
Changing darkness to color by a word;
Dividing morning, noon, and sable night.
Gathered the waters, continents appeared.
He planted vegetables and fruits to eat,
Hanging the sun and moon into the heavens.
With animals of every kind for meat,
Their skins for clothes, multiple provisions.
The light tumbled down a narrow way
Toward a hill, the derelictions of a day.

Genesis 1:1–2:3; John 1:1–18; Psalm 33:9

2

ANCESTRY OF CHRIST

Jesus, the Son of God: his ancestry
Goes back long before time began.
The Gospel writers do his family tree
To prove Jesus more than any man,
But God made flesh, come here to live with us
In Adam's dust. God sent him here to show
Love from the heart of all that ever was,
To woo us like a bridegroom who long has known
The poor, reluctant bride whom he will win
And bring home into his Father's court,
Her garments gleaming, new and sparkling clean.
He will give all to be her obedient Lord,
Even to die and be raised up to life
All for the joy of taking her to wife.

Mark 2:18–19; Hosea 2:16–20; Psalm 45:7b–9

3

JESUS' MISSION

The first couple wanted to be the last word,
To rule over their own desires and live
In Eden untempled, lords of their fallen world.
Disorder, chaos unraveled out of Eve,
Her will rampant against old Adam's will.
Suffering conflict because they disobeyed,
Wanting their way, going in for the kill.
Even their efforts to make things right just made
The tangles worse. This little one will come
To tent among us here on earth, in fact,
So all creation will be restored and home.
Keeping his Father's covenant, the pact,
He will make a heaven here, a holy place
With harmonies of light filling each space.

Genesis 3:1–20; John 1:14–18; Romans 16:20

4

THE GENEALOGY OF OUR LORD [A]

There's Abraham, too, a child of earth,
Hearing the promises of God, whose voice
Led him to leave the city of his birth
And journey far away, a happy choice.
The future opened before him, bright as the stars,
Teeming with heirs, pilgrims to a promised land
Following a cloud of smoke and light through the dark,
Their numbers exceeding even the desert sands.
Dreaming on, Jesus in his loins,
He saw fire burning at the edge of night.
The seed and promises of God were joined—
His Son and heir, gleaming as the world's true light.
By faith, Abraham wanted a better place,
Jesus, the heavenly country, the way of ways.

Matthew 1:1; Genesis 15:1–21; Hebrews 11:8–16

5

THE GENEALOGY OF OUR LORD [B]

A sorry lot of ancestors for him:
Adulterers, murderers, women of the night,
Sinners of every stripe, not one of them
Perfect. He is heir to a sinful tribe.
All this corruption Jesus' body knows,
The tangled skein of Eden: the Gordian knot
Winding itself around us in our woes
Does not ensnare him; he sees the troubled plot
Where, by the sweat of his brow, he'll set us free,
Feeling in his corpuscles the red stain
Rebellion sent spilling from a forbidden tree,
Spreading to a cross where he will be slain.
He will set things right and make things new
Unraveling every coil in the viper's brood.

Matthew 1:1–17; Genesis 3:15; Romans 5:12–21

6

THE GENEALOGY OF OUR LORD [C]

The seed of Rahab flowing in his veins
With Tamar's, Ruth's, Bathsheba's. They all seized
The red thread of salvation for their pains,
Scarlet ribbons flapping in the breeze.
All these run in our Savior's infant blood.
He'll know everything these women did,
And he will wash them in the Jordan's flood.
Nothing that ever happened will be hid.
He'll see through them, the marrow of their bones,
All they have suffered, all of the pain and hurt.
He'll bear them in his body, all alone.
Forsaken on a tree, he'll be the first
To feel their bruises in his beaten flesh,
Victim and victor tangling in his retching breath.

Matthew 1:1–6; Joshua 2:1–21; Ruth 4:13–17

7

THE NATIVITY OF JOHN

An angel beside the altar of incense stunned
Old Zechariah; his prayers hid in the smoke
Rising from the gold. Silver tongued,
His voice went mute with fear as the angel spoke:
"Fear not, rejoice, for God has heard your prayers.
Your wife, Elizabeth, will bear a son."
"Impossible, for we are up in years."
"A miracle, and you will name him John."
"How shall I know this, for I am almost dead,
My wife long past the bearing of a child."
"You'll lose the power to speak," the presence said.
Speechless with disbelief, the old man smiled.
A door that had been closed was opening up.
The old priest walked into a night of hope.

Luke 1:5–25; Genesis 18:1–15; Exodus 30:5–8

8

ANNUNCIATION

Botticelli shows us its magnitude,
The Annunciation: the book of prophecy,
The angel Gabriel kneeling, Mary in blue
And red, standing, eyes closed, what does she see
Under her heart? Between their outstretched hands,
Electric with hope, we can draw a line
Into the background where two cities stand,
A river between them, the human and divine,
A ship looking for harbor, an unfinished bridge
Over the water, an artery for God.
We wait this moment to span it ridge to ridge.
Breathless, we watch, not quite sure she will nod
Her head, while we are pointed toward the light,
To the church, past the grave, the laurel, the angel's flight.

Luke 1:26–38; Isaiah 7:14; Psalm 89:3–4

9

THE VISITATION

Like the ark holding the words of God,
Manna from heaven, safe from corruption's worm,
A flowering almond staff, old Aaron's rod,
She carries divinity; the seed takes form
Inside her flesh. The God who created all
Incarnate in a tiny human child,
One who fills the universe goes small,
Helpless, a little baby, without any guile.
John, his cousin, will recognize his Lord
Dancing inside his mother with David's joy
When Mary, bearing him, comes to the door
To visit his aged mother. The two rejoice.
Infinity confined within a human space,
Magnificats of beauty in her face.[1]

Luke 1:39–56; 1 Samuel 2:1–10; 2 Samuel 6:1–15

---

[1] Published in *Lutheran Forum* 54, no. 1 (Spring 2020): 24.

10

BIRTH AND CIRCUMCISION
OF JOHN THE BAPTIST

Mary left them; Elizabeth bore John:
An old woman suffering labor pains
Rejoicing that God had blessed them with a son;
Zechariah still mute, as the angel ordained.
Then the circumcision. Elizabeth
Gave the child its name. People frowned.
"It's not a family name!" in one breath
They shouted, then Zechariah wrote it down:
"His name is John!" His mouth opened with joy.
It frightened their neighbors in the Judean Hills.
They wondered about the birth of this little boy.
What would become of him? The gossip mills
Churned through the countryside. None of them knew
What to make of this labor now come true.

Luke 1:57–66; Genesis 18:9–15; Leviticus 12:3

11

ZECHARIAH'S SONG: THE BENEDICTUS

Zechariah, now able to speak,
Broke forth in a song as old as Israel.
Phrases he had spoken many times a week
Burst from him like waters from a deep well
As the prophetic oracles arose
In the old man's throat, blessing the Lord his God
Like King David, Ezra; benedictions flowed
Over the child, his own flesh, with awe.
It set him in the ancient prophet's place,
Pointing to the one who is to come
To free us from bondage and cry, "Prepare the way!"
Feeling the galaxies dance and hum,
The baby in his arms made the old man chant
Praises still rising to heaven from every land.

Luke 1:67–80; Ezra 7:27–28; Psalm 132:17

12

JOSEPH'S DECISION TO WED MARY

The genesis of Jesus, Matthew says,
Began when the angel Gabriel came
To visit Mary in the final days
Of her betrothal to Joseph. It brought them shame:
Pregnancy out of wedlock. He quietly planned
To put her away. The angel appeared
In a dream, filled with instructions. A good man,
Obedient to the Lord, faithful, sincere,
He did as the angel said: took Mary as wife
And cared for her, watching as her body grew
Filling out with the child, making way for life.
The hovering of the Spirit coming true
In a simple maid, a lovely country girl:
He woke to the Spirit's breathing a whole new world.

Matthew 1:18–25; Deuteronomy 22:20–22; Revelation 21:5

13

JOSEPH'S CALLING

Joseph, hearing the angel in his dream,
Knew we do not live alone. God blessed
The life growing inside Mary's womb.
Now he had duties from which he could not rest.
Mary, caught in the grasp of prophecy,
Needed his word that he would always care
For her as the child within her came to be,
Opening them to a future they now shared.
Changed by a yes from Mary, called to serve,
They were turned around. Everyone hearing the news
A child is expected must convert
And change their ways. Joseph, who would not choose
To let the child perish of his own neglect,
Turned toward a journey he did not elect.

Matthew 1:18–25; 2 Samuel 11:5; Luke 16:10

14

JOURNEY TO BETHLEHEM

Divinity made large demands on them:
Mary, pregnant, Joseph, far from kin,
Plodding their way toward Bethlehem.
Fearing how soon her labor would begin,
The stars wheeling over them, high above,
No miracles to help them, the mundane facts
Followed them down the road, no ancient god
To take them out of nature, change the ass
Into a steed riding across the sky, his wings
Fanning apocalyptic winds and fires.
No trumpets blaring that the donkey bore a king
Waiting his birth in a stable not for hire.
Into their poverty, she lay down,
Her contractions pushing a bloody crown.

Luke 2:1–7; John 7:40–44; Psalm 89:5–7

15

THE BIRTH OF JESUS

His mother wrapped him up in swaddling clothes
And laid him in a manger where cattle feed,
Waiting to feel her milk begin to flow,
Nourishment, the staff of life we need.
She saw the dark expression on his face
Scowling with hunger, bawling, gasping for air
When she picked him up. Now she is the grace
He pleads for, weeping frantic infant prayers.
One day he'll promise he's the bread of life
Come down to feed us more than food or drink,
The living water, brought from realms of light,
To satisfy our thirst. For this, we cling
To him, the sustenance he has to give.
We crave this Bethlehem so we can live.

Luke 2:1–7; John 6:47–51; Micah 5:1–5

16

THE ANGELS TO THE SHEPHERDS

The shepherds read the stars for signs and wonders
As they watched their flocks by night. Suddenly,
Out of midnight, a light blazed and thundered,
The glory of the Lord all they could see.
"Fear not," the angel sang, as they fell down
Worshipping what they did not understand.
The words washed over them in waves of sound
Phrases they knew by heart from their ancient land.
In a manger, in the city of David, the wonder lay.
The heav'ns broke open with hosts of angel choirs;
All nature shook with oracles of praise.
The shepherds ran over the hills to inquire
After the one the prophets had decreed,
The rose of Sharon lying where animals feed.

Luke 2:8–20; Isaiah 9:6–7; Galatians 4:4–5

17

THE ADORATION OF THE SHEPHERDS

The shepherds enter the stable with some sheep
Who always appear in the paintings. The ox and ass
Are grinning because they know this babe asleep
Is their God, reading what has come to pass.
In the tableaus, the child is bathed in light,
His mother worshipping him, and Joseph stunned.
The shepherds, rural and awed, Jesus in their sight.
What is this marvel that our God has done?
All the pomp and circumstance of stars
And now in this rough-hewn stable they find the child,
Creator of all, innocent and poor.
They kneel in wonder, hearing his infant cry.
Drawn to his side, they feel solid ground move,
A poor baby reaching out for our love.

Luke 2:8–20; Isaiah 1:2–3; Micah 5:2–5

18

THE CIRCUMCISION AND NAMING OF JESUS

This cut drew the first blood of our Lord,
Submitting to the Law, the Holy One,
To show the covenant in flesh and blood,
Now Son of Joseph, who took him as his own,
Naming him Jesus, as Pharaoh's daughter named
Moses, drawing him out of the river Nile.
All righteousness fulfilled, our Lord became
What he was meant to be, his Father's child
Come to redeem the world, to live with us
Obeying all the ordinary rules.
For what? To bleed and die upon a cross,
To show us how he is the God of fools
And sages. A god incarnate, filled with life.
And so we watch with wonder, the hand, the knife.

Luke 2:21; Genesis 17:9–13; Exodus 2:1–11

19

THE PURIFICATION OF MARY

Forty days after the birth, Mary came
For the purification, a ritual bath.
Two turtledoves for the sacrificial flame.
All births fill women with thoughts of death.
We see in her eyes a new wisdom found,
Knowing the frantic push toward life can kill,
The weariness of labor, then the sound
Of the new soul at the edge of heaven or hell.
Did she weep as he passed through the watery door,
Knowing that she had made it and would not die,
Crying joyful praises to her Lord:
"Thanks for saving me, the sacrifice
Bringing me back to huswifery again
Through the horned gates never breached by men."

Luke 2:22–27; Exodus 13:1–2; Leviticus 12:1–8

20

MARY AT THE PRESENTATION OF JESUS

Daughter of Eve, fresh as Eden, she looked
Sweetly at Jesus. No longer innocent,
Now wife and mother, holding him in the crook
Of her arm while she fed him, capable, content
Trying to read his lips for signs without words.
Every new mother looks at her child to see
Portents of great things, a Savior of the world,
But now just a girl handing him to the priest.
She knew the prophets and smiled as the baby cried.
A second Adam, the maker of all things
Incarnate, as the old man prophesied
That God had chosen her, the one to bring
Into the world a breath that once had breathed
Over the waters to make a world complete.

Luke 2:33–36; Genesis 1:1–2; Isaiah 52:10

21

SIMEON'S SONG

He lay in Simeon's arms, straining to raise
His head, heir to the cosmos, the royal line,
Uncomprehending of the old man's praise.
The mother, fresh as a bud, knew the signs,
Rapt in the old man's words, his prophecy,
Flinching at the sword he saw piercing her heart.
Joseph offered two turtledoves decreed
By the law for the poor at the formal rite.
They stood there, washed in the colors drifting around,
Hearing a song that meant the old man's death,
A grand farewell, the evening light going down,
Hope shining around him, golden, his raspy breath
Telling the world that here was the little Son
Creation, history, the ending, all in one.

Luke 2:28–35; Isaiah 49:6; Acts 13:47–49

22

THE PROPHETESS ANNA

Barren, she lived dreaming that God would hear
Her prayers, like Hannah or Elizabeth,
Waiting each month for the blood not to appear.
Each time it came, she suffered a little death.
Her husband died, his bones in his father's vault,
No one to care for, no one to walk her way.
Childless, a woman whose tears were more than salt.
Widowed, she married the temple, night and day
Fasting and praying, expectant in faith and hope,
Believing that the promise would bear fruit.
When Simeon's song burst out, her heart leaped up,
A poor couple with a baby, the very truth,
Ordinary earth, old Sarah's son
Born to her, bright as the morning of Eden's dawn.

Luke 2:36–38; 2 Chronicles 34:22–28; 1 Timothy 5:3–5

23

THE STAR OF BETHLEHEM

They followed its journey over the sandy hills
Leading them forward into the setting sun.
They knew the signs and read their planets well;
Conjunctions in the heavens led them on.
For they believed in portents from the sky
That made them pack their bags and travel west.
They did not know nor could they fathom why,
An ancient puzzle burning within their heads.
They trusted prophecy to tell the truth,
Laboring over each page of the ancient books
That drew their camels into the windy blue,
Over the drifting desert way they took.
All the world rode with them, from near and far,
Tracking the riddles in a brilliant star.

Matthew 2:1–12; Numbers 24:17; Revelation 22:16

24

THE VISIT OF THE MAGI

They brought gold, frankincense, and myrrh,
Gifts for this newborn king in Bethlehem.
They followed all the rules, causing a stir
In Herod's palace in Jerusalem.
A king? Wary of any royal threat,
The tyrant questioned the wise men where he lived.
Sages, they knew his pious, sweet request
Was bloody, any advice that he could give,
His powers impotent before the Lord.
They knew this child filled them with cosmic joy,
The galaxies dancing as never before.
They found him with Mary. Kneeling before the boy,
They worshipped him whom they could not betray.
Returning, rejoicing they knew a better way.

Matthew 2:1–12; Daniel 2:12–23; Psalm 72:10–14

25

THE FLIGHT INTO EGYPT

The angel appeared again to Joseph, "Go!
Flee to Egypt with Mary and the child!
Herod is mad with terror. Do not be slow!
Flee on your donkey to the river Nile.
Like Abraham, you'll find refuge there,
Safe from the soldier's sword, the killer's blade.
Eat of the corn, the fleshpots, exotic fare.
Relish the palm trees; rest in their shade.
Portents of sorrow, the shadows on the moon
Will flit around your head like scavenging birds,
Ravens circling the carcasses of doom."
He woke from the dream, heeding the angel's words.
With the child, the weary couple fled
To save him for another death instead.

Matthew 2:13–15; Genesis 12:10–16; Hosea 11:1

26

THE MASSACRE OF THE INNOCENTS

Innocents died for Jesus on that day,
Crimson with Herod's jealousies. Wrath
Sweeping across the land where toddlers played,
Now in the way of Herod's killing path.
Mothers and sisters shrieking against the devil,
Weeping like Rachel over their absent sons.
Herod, playing the part of sin and evil,
Wreaked vengeance on children for what God had done.
Refusing to be comforted, they wept,
Forever having lost their future peace.
Grief overcame them. They could not forget
The ruthless tyrant's beastly cruelties.
Grasping the tiny fingers of their boys
Stiffened by death as Herod's bloody toys.

Matthew 2:16–18; Exodus 1:15–22; Jeremiah 31:15

27

THE DEATH OF KING HEROD THE GREAT

Herod the Great, cunning, cruel, no good,
Died in agony, cursing, and all alone.
A brutal tyrant, wallowing in blood,
His children's, anyone's, to keep his throne,
Trying to please the Hebrew God and Lord,
Rebuilding the temple in Jerusalem.
His worship curved into himself; his sword
Murdered pretenders, babies in Bethlehem.
The wise men knew he was a king to fear
And tricked him, going home by another way.
Like all monarchs who refuse to hear
Another king is born, they rule the day
And slaughter him. It takes away our breath;
All earthly kingdoms fall to the lance of death.

Matthew 2:16–21; Exodus 4:19; Psalm 2:1–12

28

JESUS GOES WITH HIS
FAMILY TO NAZARETH

A second Israel, he follows the patriarchs
Fleeing to Egypt for safety, health, and food
Into oblivion, out of the way, gone dark,
Like a crucifixion absent the cruel wood,
Descending, and then a second Exodus,
Up like Moses, out of the watery sea.
Jesus riding a donkey north for us;
Joseph rehearsing ancient prophecies.
Out of his mouth like Samuel's, words of old
Will come as yet unspoken deeds that fly
Into the place where promises unfold,
The recesses that flash before our eyes:
Jesus, a Nazarite, Mary's son,
Dying to make us all his holy ones.

Matthew 2:19–23; Genesis 46:1–7; Exodus 4:19

29

FINDING JESUS IN THE TEMPLE

They thought him with his cousins and their kin;
Suddenly, they knew his presence was not there.
Panic scattered them, looking for him.
Frantic, for three days, searching everywhere.
A boy of twelve. How could they leave him behind?
And then they found him in his Father's house.
There in the temple they rejoiced to find
Jesus alive and well. But still they groused:
"How could you do this? We were worried sick!"
Mary pondered, What could all this mean?
The thought of losing him hurt to the quick.
We wonder where our God and Lord has been.
He is in his temple, never far away.
We have abandoned *him* and gone astray.

Luke 2:41–52; Exodus 23:14–17; 1 Samuel 2:18–26

Part Two

THE public ministry of Jesus

The Preparation for Jesus' Ministry

30

LAMB OF GOD

"Behold the Lamb of God!" cried John, pointing
At one who would take away the sins of the world.
His two disciples followed Christ, joining
Together with hundreds who believed his words.
Here was Messiah standing in their midst.
"What do you want?" he asked. "Where are you staying?"
"Come and see," he told them, "where I live."
He made a place for them, his invitation
Standing open for his beloved guests.
He is our dwelling, God's temple here on earth,
The one who makes us feel at home and blessed;
The life of the party dying to give us birth.
They stayed with him, then followed at his side
That one day would be pierced and gaping wide.

John 1:29–39; Matthew 3:1–12; Isaiah 40:3–5

31

BAPTISM OF JESUS

His best man for the nuptials will be John,
Preaching and baptizing in Jordan's springs.
The last of the prophets, with next to nothing on,
Camel suit, a leather belt, no ring,
No tie, no wedding garment, really odd.
Elijah's second coming, John points Christ out,
Telling us all, "Behold, the Lamb of God!"
He stands in the river as he shouts,
"After me comes one greater than I!"
The water rushing, dappled with floods of light,
Washing us clean, words falling from the sky:
Over his head, a sound, a dove taking flight,
Tearing the heav'ns open, igniting the flame,
Kindling the morning sun, the thunder's name.

Mark 1:1–11; 2 Kings 1:8; Isaiah 64:1–2

32

TEMPTATION OF JESUS [A]

A Moabite, Ruth's family was a mess:
All the way back to Lot and his daughters' tricks
To keep their heritage, they both transgressed,
Conceiving Ammon and Moab just in the nick
Of time, all of this tangled in Jesse's line.
It shows Christ's legacy of human guilt,
Transgressions, failures, offenses combined.
The Son of David's spirit cannot wilt.
He will fight this Goliath, battle his hoard.
Into the desert he goes, to the tempter's lair,
Defeating the devil's plot to be his lord,
Mocking his pious talk and evil prayers
To test his will against the devil's wiles,
The prince of darkness with his gilt-edged spoils.

Matthew 4:1–2; Genesis 19:30–38; Deuteronomy 9:9

33

TEMPTATION OF JESUS [B]

He fasted forty days and forty nights.
Weak with hunger, Jesus needed food.
Something hissed in the sand, "You need a bite?
Bake some bread out of stones, then you can prove
You're real. Your dad sent manna down to eat
And fed your people forty years. Say the word!
Don't just stand here in this desert heat,
Do something! Cook dinner; be a Lord!"
Mirages of food rise in the rippling air.
A second Adam lifts his scruffy heel,
Stepping on a voice speaking from anywhere,
Making to crush his head for a handsome meal.
He smiles, "Man does not live by bread alone,"
Sucking the marrow out of old Nick's bones.

Matthew 4:3–4; Deuteronomy 8:1–6; Hebrews 2:18

34

TEMPTATION OF JESUS [C]

The Devil quotes Scripture, knows its ins and outs.
"Fall down and prove you are God's only Son.
Let the angels catch you, or do you doubt
Your Father's word, 'Your foot will not hit a stone.'?"
Cagey, making Jesus say God lies.
"Pray, step out in the air, fall to the earth.
Believe, even if it means you'll die."
Here on the highest pinnacle of church,
He asks for signs. "Show us the Father, Lord!"
Over and over we ask for living proof,
Abracadabra, magic, a swallowed sword,
Sleight of hand, not the living truth,
A hidden thing that will not show its face
But works the miracle, the means of grace.

Matthew 4:5–7; Deuteronomy 6:16–19; Psalm 91:11–12

35

TEMPTATION OF JESUS [D]

"All the kingdoms of the world," he said,
Offering our Lord power if he would bow down
And worship him. We all hung by a thread.
Would this new Adam fall again? The sound
Of galaxies stopped till the answer came.
He would not break his Father's heart to own
The worlds that he created in his name,
Going for glories only thugs have known.
Creation stopped, and then its heart resumed
Beating. He refused. The planets wheeled,
Music in their spheres, the desert bloomed,
All of the heavens danced old country reels.
Angels came down to serve him plates of food.
He looked around and saw that it was good.

Matthew 4:8–11; Deuteronomy 6:13–15; Psalm 24:1–2

36

JOHN POINTS

His bony finger always points to Christ,
The Lamb of God, who takes away the sin
Of the world. Standing in his camel suit, he cries,
"Make straight the way of the Lord!" And so begins
The ministry of Jesus. John teaches us
Who Jesus is and how we are to preach—
Get out of the way is what a preacher does
So people turn to Christ and hear him teach;
Who, seeing his true godliness in flesh,
Can fall in love with him and change their ways,
Following him past the portals of sin and death
Into the light, the end of all their days,
Glad for the voice that turned their lives around,
Grateful for the glory in the wild man's sound.

John 1:19–34; Genesis 22:8; 2 Kings 1:8; Isaiah 40:3

Jesus' Ministry until His Appearance as a Prophet

37

FIRST DISCIPLES OF JESUS

Doubting Nathanael scoffed at his brother's words,
"I've seen Messiah! Jesus of Nazareth!"
He knew the local gossip; he had heard
Nothing good came from it, like death
To live there, the end of the world, a two-bit town.
Filled with conventions, he is not prepared
When Jesus calls him. He hears a deeper sound:
Prophecy riding on provincial air.
He feels the truth proving away all fraud.
Pedestrian as dross, his soul awakes,
Cleansing his sight, "Rabbi! Son of God!"
His eyes open. He sees dimensions break:
Raptures of angels descending and ascending.
Jesus, Jacob's ladder, down from the heavens.

John 1:43–51; Genesis 28:10–22; Psalm 2:7

38

WEDDING AT CANA

His mother knew he could help all by himself
Filling the six stone water jars with wine.
The only ones who knew it were the help.
The steward marveled, the vintage aged and fine
As the party rocking and reeling in the room
Imbibed a joy they'd never drunk before,
The house spinning around the bride and groom.
This is the rite of Eden, the temple door,
When God engages with us, husbands and wives,
So two together engender another one.
He blesses them, their bodies, as they rise,
Dancing within their flesh: daughters and sons.
A miracle of joy that Jesus brings
To be our bridegroom, flagons of light to drink.

John 2:1–12; 2 Chronicles 4:5; Amos 9:13–15

39

FIRST TEMPLE CLEANSING

Fresh from his mother's house, Jesus will stride
Into the temple, the place his Father dwells,
Snapping a thick whip of cords. He will drive
The farmers out, the livestock they would sell.
Fury and rage will consume him; he will burn
With zeal, upending the boxes of pagan coins.
Thus he will cleanse us on the day he returns.
Three days and this scion of David's loins
Will raise up the marble of his body, the place
His Father now abides, and build the temple
With living stones shaped by the Father's grace.
It soon will be finished, plain and simple,
And we will be changed enough to bear the sight
Of God in flesh transfigured into light.

John 2:13–25; Malachi 3:1–3; Psalm 69:5–12

40

JESUS AND NICODEMUS [A]

He comes by night; we see him scurry in,
Afraid he will be seen. The Savior waits
Calmly for Nicodemus to begin:
"Rabbi," he calls him, and in this title states
The truth. "Teacher, we know you are from heaven;
The water turns to wine at your command.
You heal the sick, calling out the demon,
As only a god can do. Out of your hand
Bread for the hungry, water that slakes all thirst."
Then Jesus points up to the whirling spheres,
"To know me is to want a second birth."
He cannot catch a glimpse of what he hears.
The weary scholar nodding, looking down,
Misses the face with starlight dancing around.

John 3:1–21; 1 Corinthians 2:10b–16; Romans 6:4

41

JESUS AND NICODEMUS [B]

There in the night he will utter the saving verse,
"For God so loved the world he gave his Son,"
The Gospel for us in a few short words,
Written on the wind as long as the ages run.
People will remember this and find
Peace for their souls—Jesus has come for love.
He searches everywhere for us, to shine
Light in our darkness bright as the sun above.
He gives up everything and empties out
His godliness, and as he is lifted up,
Divinity splashes on the ground.
For love, he will drink this deadly cup
To give us life, eternal life with him,
And bring us home to his new Jerusalem.

John 3:16–21; Romans 5:6–11; Titus 3:3–8

42

LAST TESTIMONY OF JOHN

Like the waters pouring from the Baptist's hands,
Joy sparkles in his words of love and praise
For the bridegroom. John rejoices that he stands
Beside him at the nuptials, happy to raise
A toast to his friend. His joy is now complete:
The bridegroom has appeared; he will rejoice.
It's time for him to decrease and Christ increase.
Glad to be the one giving voice
To the heav'ns come down in flesh to make a home,
To tabernacle here, so we can live
Filled with the measures of love no one had known
Until he templed here on earth to give
Our flesh new birth from the heav'ns above,
Born for the wedding banquet of his love.

John 3:22–36; Isaiah 61:10–11; 1 John 5:12–13

43

THE SAMARITAN WOMAN
AT THE WELL [A]

Parched from his journey, Jesus sat down to think
Beside Jacob's well. Fresh water splashed
On the dusty stones. He said, "Give me a drink.
I am thirsty." "Why?" the woman asked.
Betrothals at biblical wells informed them both.
The Light of the World, the living water danced,
As the Son of God sat plighting his troth,
Now made flesh in his human glance.
All that she ever wanted—she wanted much—
Sitting beside her in the noonday heat
Wedded to words she could drink and even touch.
He saw right through her, more than the eye could see.
Rivers flowed out of his speech, a living spring;
A tall drink of water, he knew everything.

John 4:1–15; Genesis 24:10–49; Genesis 29:1–14

44

THE SAMARITAN WOMAN
AT THE WELL [B]

High noon, she went alone, when others rest,
Avoiding the crowds that came in the late afternoon.
There she found Jesus—the disciples were impressed.
Alone with a woman, you can hear them swoon.
He sounded the depth of law for those in need,
Made wine of water, cleansed the temple square,
Showed Nicodemus things he could not see,
The woman truths she found the grace to bear.
He spoke, his light blanking the sunlight out:
The great I AM, courting a worldly bride,
Speaking with words turning the spheres around.
He touched her shame, making her whole inside.
Filled with his waters, she could not wait to tell
Others, "Come, fathom the springs in Jacob's well!"

John 4:16–27; Isaiah 61:10–11; Romans 6:23

45

THE SAMARITAN WOMAN
RETURNS TO THE CITY

Beautiful, likely barren, the woman ran
Like a missionary to tell everyone,
Preaching with joy, "Come and see a man
Who told me everything I've ever done!
Is he the Messiah? Could it really be?"
All of them knew her and her fruitless past,
That men desired her was clear to see.
Would Jesus be the sixth? News travels fast.
Many followed to hear him for themselves.
He stood by the empty water jar,
A river of life rushing from his well,
Puzzling his disciples with chewy metaphors,
Proverbs of harvesting the ripened wheat
Garnered to give them seasoned fruits to eat.

John 4:28–38; Job 23:12; Isaiah 9:3

46

I HAVE NO FOOD BUT TO
DO THE WILL OF GOD

From the living water to the living bread,
Jesus turns, baffling them once more.
What he says seems nonsense; How is he fed?
Has he eaten? Did someone go to the store?
Jesus chews on miraculous food.
It satisfies him to do God's will.
The Samaritans listening quickly understood
Who he was, the disciples, troubled still—
The fields are white to harvest, time to reap.
He gave a Great Commission to them all;
Even the woman knew she had to preach,
Gathering in believers with her call.
Already the harvest milled around the Word—
Food for the Gentiles threshed for a hungry world.

John 4:31–38; Job 23:12; Joel 2:28–29

47

TESTIMONIES ABOUT JESUS

I believe because my mom and dad
Taught me to, sitting beside me with the book,
Stories about Jesus, a baby, a little lad.
Egermeier's pictures with their faded look.
Later, I met him on my own, an old friend
I had known for years. He was the same,
Though I had changed to better comprehend
His suffering and his death for me, the frame
That gave depth of perspective to my life.
He lived beside me, like food I ate and drank.
So the Samaritans when they arrived
Asked Jesus home with them and being frank
Told the woman they had heard him for themselves
And believed him, grateful she'd brought them to the well.

John 4:39–42; Deuteronomy 6:4–9; 2 Timothy 1:3–7

48

JESUS HEALS THE SON OF
THE NOBLEMAN

He knew Christ turned the water into wine.
"Now turn my son from death to life," he pled.
"I trust that you can save this boy of mine.
Come to my home before the child is dead.
The apple of my eye, more dear than gold.
For I believe in you, that you can heal."
Jesus marveled, "Your son has been made whole.
Sit down with him, embrace him, have a meal.
The fever left the boy this hour at one."
At this, the man believed with all his heart.
The servants told him; he ran to hold his son.
Faith in the Lord, never the slightest doubt,
A treasure richer than all that he possessed,
The future in his arms, whole and blest.

John 4:46–54; 1 Kings 17:21–24; Acts 16:25–34

49

JOHN THE BAPTIST IS
THROWN INTO PRISON

Herod's troubled conscience spoke for him.
Hearing of Jesus, he remembered John,
Whom he had killed. Herod felt guilty as sin
But unrepentant for the things he'd done.
He'd gladly heard John speak, knew he was right,
Even the accusations against his lusts.
Locking him up to keep him out of sight,
Fearing the multitude's wrath and breaking trust
With them, convicted by what John had preached:
The Baptist pointing clearly at Herod's crime.
The allegations that he made reached
Into his soul, salt on a wound, in time
Making him mad but feeling in John's assault
The truth stinging his soul like a dash of salt.

Matthew 14:1–5; Leviticus 18:16; Proverbs 10:17

50

PARALYTIC AT BETHESDA

An angel descends; water splashes up
Out of the pool. Around it lie the sick
Waiting for a touch, hoping against hope
Someone will help him. Bitter to the quick,
Accusing others where he found their fault—
No one reaches to help; he cherishes his pain.
Hobbled to his hurts, he fears a fall
All of the changes if he should walk again.
He dreads the consequence of being healed,
Standing again, in the temple square
Where miracles are spoken of and sealed.
An invalid made whole again by prayer,
Christ's words will tear his ill defense apart,
Plunging God into his crippled heart.

John 5:1–18; Nehemiah 3:1; Psalm 72:12–14

Jesus' Ministry as the Prophet of Galilee

51

RETURN OF JESUS TO GALILEE

Jesus now withdrew to Galilee,
Out of the way. The prophets had foretold
His going to Capernaum by the sea
To those who sat in great darkness, once sold
Into bondage, slaves to the lords of Babylon.
Now light bursts through the torpor of the night.
He will take up the ministry of John,
Preaching that the kingdom of God is nigh.
And in his body, the temple he will build
That cannot be corrupted by our sin.
Now he has come, a human being filled
With the Spirit, robed in God's luster, without, within.
Telling the Galileans to turn around,
Change their ways and beat the devil down.

Matthew 4:12–25; Isaiah 9:1–2; 1 Corinthians 1:26–28

52

JESUS CALLS TWO PAIRS OF BROTHERS

Jesus went into the boat to teach the crowd
With Simon, Andrew, James, John and their nets
After a poor time fishing. They'd been out
Through the night and caught nothing, yet
He charged them, "Go to deep waters; let down
Your nets," his voice urging them to go
Past the far banks where fish are rarely found:
A catch of silver riches filled their hold.
Peter sank to his knees, "Go away!
I am a sinful man." Jesus said,
"I am the miracle come to make
Disciples rich in faith, to raise the dead."
They left their boats to follow him for life.
A sentence netting fish without a price.

Luke 5:1–11; Ezekiel 47:9–10; John 21:4–8

53

EXORCISM AT THE SYNAGOGUE
IN CAPERNAUM

Jesus walked into the synagogue
For prayers. Suddenly, all hell broke loose:
A shriek, "We know you, Holy Son of God!"
The fiend panicked; it knew what Christ would do.
His very presence cast the demons out.
The man thrashed around on the dusty floor,
Then stillness. All the people could talk about
Was how his words drove it out the door
Into the wild landscapes of Galilee,
How he routed the enemy, cleansed the man.
He comes from a world our vision cannot see
But we should listen for, if we can,
When Jesus brings it near. We hear it thrum
In earth's foundations as the kingdom comes.

Luke 4:31–37; Acts 19:15–17; James 2:19

54

HEALING THE MOTHER
OF PETER'S WIFE

Without a prayer, he saw her, touched her hand.
The raging fever left her; she got up
And served the Lord with gratitude. A man
Breaking the rituals with more than a cup
Of cool water; her illness vanished. He healed
A woman, like the leper, out of bounds.
His kingdom opens into miracles
When he is near. She came around
Able to do what she had always done:
Make dinner for them all, their gathered friends.
A big deal. A woman cooks for her son,
Slipping into something new that ends
Her station, topples and overturns the old.
No ordinary here: a world unscrolled.

Matthew 8:14–17; Isaiah 53:4; Revelation 21:5

55

JESUS JOURNEYS THROUGH GALILEE AND PREACHES

Like a hospital ward, people in beds,
Faces vacant from chills and fevers, they lie
Too ill for hope, not quite living or dead;
Demons shrieking his name. Stopping their cry
And touching them, he draws the sickness out
Into himself, nursing as his own
Each sorrow, every pain; there is no doubt
He is God's Son; the spirits wail and moan.
His word captures them, puts them in a bind—
All is made new, like Eden's seventh day,
God enjoying the evening in his mind,
Everything fresh again as early May.
He will redeem with his body all our hurts,
A new Adam, heaven shaped out of earth.

Matthew 4:23–24; Psalm 103:1–5; 1 Corinthians 15:45–47

56

A LESSON IN PRAYER

Our God is like a friend whom we disturb,
Rousing him in the middle of the night
Asking for bread, three loaves. Jesus observes
What he does—he rises, lights the light,
And finds the loaf because he is good,
Not because we are persistent. We can keep
Pestering, be unmannerly with God,
Interrupting what we think is sleep.
God will not mind that we disturbed his rest
To do our bidding and listens when we come
To tell him what we need, make our request,
Bothering him, with his children in bed at home.
He will get up and answer our frantic prayer.
An emblem of God, a figure beyond compare!

Luke 11:5–8; Psalm 50:14–15; James 1:5

57

ASK AND YOU WILL RECEIVE

Jesus says, to be rich, we must learn to beg,
Asking for what we need, seeking to find,
Knocking so doors are opened, knowing the check
Is in the mail, keeping God in mind.
Our fulsome praises do not hold the charm
But sharing like friends all we would receive,
Shunning modesty, asking for the farm.
Living in a faithful trust where we believe
God wants to make us rich in what is good
And is able to give worlds of treasures away,
Waiting only until we've understood
Our breathing in and out is how we pray.
Opening our hearts for the heritage we hold.
Reveling in our wealth. Prayer makes us bold.

Luke 11:9–13; 2 Chronicles 15:2–4; 1 John 3:22

58

WHAT IT MEANS TO FOLLOW JESUS

Jesus sees right through us; he listens to
The things we say and understands our bent.
A scribe wants to follow him and do
Some teaching, in his own element,
And go with Jesus everywhere; he means
Work in his company. Jesus says,
"I have no home office and wander between
Cities and villages teaching a better way."
Another offers to follow him, but not just yet:
"I must bury my father." Jesus tells
Him, "Follow me, the dead can bury the dead."
Jesus speaks the truth; he reads us well,
Showing us discipleship has costs,
Which only the world could mark up as loss.

Matthew 8:18–22; Psalm 40:17; 1 Corinthians 7:29–31

59

THE STORM AT SEA

Exhausted, Jesus boarded a small boat,
Falling to sleep on a cushion in the stern.
A gale came up—they could hardly keep afloat
Bailing out the water as the waves churned—
While Jesus slept like Jonah in the ship.
"Teacher, don't you care that we will die?"
They cried and woke him up, hearing the boards rip
Apart. He rebuked the winds and cried,
"Peace, be still!" The winds ceased; a great calm
Spread over the waters. "Why are you afraid?
Where is your faith?" The words of the mariner's psalm
Rode on the rolling main as the storm obeyed
Its master. His powers dawning on them, fear
Sank them into terror as their God came clear.

Mark 4:35–41; Psalm 107:23–32; Jonah 1:4–9

60

HEALING THE GERASENE DEMONIAC

The stormy sea calmed, now a wild man,
A legion of demons, barges out of the graves;
Screaming in fury, they know him, understand
Who he is. The Son of God! They rant and rave.
His powers draw their spirits out in fear;
They know he is their end, that they will die.
His very presence brings the kingdom near,
And so they foment spirits in the sky.
"Send us into the swine!" Jesus says, "Go!"
A herd of pigs plunges into the sea,
Water undoes them, drowned by its undertow
They perish. Possessed no longer, he is free
To follow Jesus. Unloosed, he has new work:
Raise from these ghostly sepulchers a church.

Matthew 8:28–34; 2 Peter 2:4–5; Revelation 20:9–10

61

HEALING THE PARALYTIC
AT CAPERNAUM

Jesus at home, overwhelmed by disease,
Sick people on beds blocking the Savior's door;
Four men carrying a friend, without saying please,
Break through the roof, lowering him to the floor
In front of Jesus, who marvels at their faith!
It moves him to say, "Son, your sins are forgiven!"
The theologians watching are dismayed.
"Who gave our hometown boy the keys to heaven?
Only God can forgive our sins," they jeer.
Sin was the root of the paralytic's woe;
God's holiness itself would work the cure.
Jesus banks on the laws his Father wrote.
When he says, "Rise up, my son, and walk!"
He rose, proving his words are more than talk.

Matthew 9:1–8; Job 42:1–6; Acts 14:8–15

62

CALLING OF MATTHEW

"Follow me," he says, and Matthew leaves
His job with all its perks behind: the things
Money could buy, all that he believed,
Making him richer than some petty kings.
He earned their hatred; it seemed worth the price.
Then a voice out of the depths called to him,
Like a healing balm flowing from paradise,
Soothing the hurts that all Capernaum
Levied for him in wounds he could not cure.
His duties called him to losses beyond his ken.
He needed the oil of mercy spread on the hurts
That he had suffered in the eyes of men.
Light overhead shines on his dazzled face
When Jesus calls him to spend his wealth with grace.

Matthew 9:9–13; Proverbs 21:3; 1 Timothy 1:12–15

63

AT MATTHEW'S HOUSE

Tax collectors, Matthew and his friends,
Jesus, the disciples, enjoying dinner.
The religious wanted to know what it meant
For him to carouse with outcasts, whores, and sinners.
"Scripture says, keep yourself apart!"
But he knows death has set his teeth in us.
Jesus came to heal our broken hearts,
Going to be the doctor at Matthew's house.
He is the medicine everybody needs,
The Great Physician come to make us whole.
He visits the squalor where we live to treat
All of our ailments, body, mind, and soul:
We are like patients in a waiting room
Hoping against hope he will check our doom.

Matthew 9:9–13; Hosea 6:6; Micah 6:8

64

NEW WINE INTO OLD WINESKINS

The fast ended; bridesmaids rejoice with the bride
As they help to celebrate her wedding day.
Her long dress rustles behind her; she glows with pride
As her groom smiles. He has come from far away
To take her back to his father's house,
Where they will live forever. He brings good cheer,
Splurging on food and wine; they dance, carouse,
Waltzing into the future, for spring is here.
Like new wine being poured into a skin,
It gushes forth with joy into their hearts
Made new by grace so life can begin again.
Poured into old hearts, it would split them apart.
The bridegroom comes with joy to fill our glass
Up to the brim, rejoice. Winter is past!

Mark 2:19–22; Song of Songs 1:4; Hebrews 8:13

65

RAISING THE DAUGHTER OF
JAIRUS FROM THE DEAD

Jairus trusted Jesus could help him out.
His daughter was at home dying. His pleas
Told the whole story; without a doubt,
Faith sounded loud and clear, "Come, follow me!"
Jesus followed the man to his home,
Where flutes and mourners weeping to high heaven
Told him she was dead; he should have come
Earlier—no nostrums could now be given
To save her. Jesus called her death a sleep.
Laughing loudly, they cried there was no hope.
They were paid to mourn, to wail and weep.
Death was their living, but Jesus raised her up
Out of a dreamless world where darkness reigned
Into the fields of morning where light obtained.

Mark 5:21–23, 35–43; Psalm 33:9; 2 Timothy 4:2

66

HEALING THE BLEEDING WOMAN

For twelve years the blood had flowed; she'd paid
Countless doctors, experts to purchase help
And nothing. Still unclean, day after day,
Only the Great Physician could make her well.
She thought, "If I could only touch the fringe
Of his garment, I'd be healed, made whole again."
She bolted her way in, grabbed his robe. The hinge
Of the universe swung open. Like lightning, it trained
Through her; she felt the leakage stop from the inside.
He turned and asked, "Who touched me? I could feel
A charge leave me." The woman did not hide.
In shock, she fell down, her body healed.
"Your faith has made you well. Go in peace."
Her thanks streamed from her body, the issue ceased.

Mark 5:25–34; Exodus 15:26; Leviticus 15:25–30

67

TWO BLIND MEN AT GALILEE

Jesus goes to his home so he can be
Alone, in peace and quiet, away from the crowds.
"Son of David!" they cry, "Help us see!"
They name him Messiah openly and loud,
Barging right in. "Have mercy on us," they pray.
What kind of faith draws them into his house?
Enough to come inside, to make their way.
He looks at their eyes, weeping with blood and pus,
And reaches to touch them with his human hands.
The darkness clears. Suddenly, they see the light.
"Keep it a secret" is his only demand.
Stunned by the flash of images in their eyes,
They run, disobedient, into town
Telling each person they meet: God has come down!

Matthew 9:27–31; Psalm 146:8; Isaiah 29:18

68

EXORCISING A MAN WHO WAS MUTE

His friends believed and brought him to the Lord,
Who, casting out his demon, gave him speech.
What he said, Matthew did not record,
But people marveled, mercies they'd never seen;
Where did he get those powers? Some said the devil.
Shocking. Here is a man able to turn
Lives around with a touch. This is not evil.
No matter what we skeptics have learned
About miracles, would we have praised
God or grumbled at this madman who broke the rules,
Even the codes our current scribes have phrased?
Could we bear to be numbered among the fools
Who took their friend to Jesus to be healed,
Astonished as the learned doctors reeled?

Matthew 9:32–34; 2 Kings 1:2–4; Psalm 103:1–5

69

EXORCISING THE BLIND
AND MUTE MAN

Jesus heals the man possessed and blind.
He speaks; they marvel. "Is this King David's Son?"
It drives the theologians out of their minds.
Who can this be? We've never seen this done!
He must be of the devil; they are all
Opposing him, a battle of estates:
"A kingdom divided against itself will fall.
Enemies will attack; they will lay it waste."
He fights with evil, not against himself.
Whose soldier am I? Would I have said he's God
Or devilish? This is about faith and nothing else.
A war is raging; there is no middle spot:
For when the miracle was coming true
Believers saw what skeptics never knew.

Matthew 12:22–28; Deuteronomy 7:15; Hebrews 12:28

70

PARABLE OF THE STRONG MAN

Have you ever—? Jesus is the thief
Shackling the strong man down to plunder his house,
The devil's, prince of this world, the grim chief
Of sorrow, he who scatters evil about,
Bringing his chaos into our domain,
Prowling around to ruin what is right.
Christ has bound him in thick chains to reclaim
All of the spoils he ransacked in the night,
To make our hearts orderly and clean,
Where sunlight spills into the window squares,
Shining on snowy lilies and leaves of green,
And keepsakes like the family silverware
Are safe even if we hear the clink
Of irons in the den where the demon slinks.

Mark 3:27; Isaiah 49:24–25; 1 John 5:10

71

THE SIGN OF JONAH

Like Jonah, he will preach, but they'll want signs,
Proof that he speaks for God, that he comes from heaven.
He will rebuke them for being two-faced and blind
And answer any argument they've given.
Then he will enter into the heart of earth
Like the prophet in the belly of the whale,
Dying to live, the fish spewing him forth,
A man turned around, no longer turning tail.
Like him going down from his gaping tomb
To harrow the fundaments of death and hell,
Bringing the devil's battlements their doom,
Ending the tyranny where Satan dwells,
Cleansing his church of disbelief and sin,
Driving them out and bringing his kingdom in.

Matthew 12:38–42; Jonah 2:1; 1 Peter 4:6

72

JESUS' TRUE RELATIVES

Jesus, whose blood ran in David's line,
Always refused to do his family tree.
One with his Father in heaven, under his sign,
He resisted relatives. His destiny:
To be our older brother, in the end
Binding us to himself so he could make
Sisters and brothers, mothers, lifelong friends
Of the lost whose hearts are hurt, ready to break,
All new relations adopted by his word;
God's love made flesh and blood to make us his.
He fathers us and will not be deterred:
Drowning us in the waters of all that is
To raise us as his own doing his will,
Engraving on our flesh the family seal.

Mark 3:31–35; Deuteronomy 33:19; Romans 8:12–17

Parables of the Kingdom

73

PARABLE OF THE SOWER [A]

He was the dwelling that his hearers sought,
The temple of the most high God in flesh.
They crowded around his home to hear him talk
In images that sprang into something fresh.
His words constructed new realities
With heaven's timbers building up a house,
A mansion gleaming beside a glassy sea
Crystal and shining, refracting every doubt.
In him, we have a cosmic carpenter
Making a boat, a nave, in which we sail
While waves of sound grow in our fertile ears.
A kingdom breaks in on a summer gale
Over the waters; parables for seeds,
Their syllables growing faster than the weeds.

Matthew 13:3–9; Isaiah 55:10–11; Revelation 21:22–27

74

PARABLE OF THE SOWER [B]

A sower goes out to sow and scatters seeds
On the sidewalk. They cannot grow. The birds come
And snatch them up. They are like Satan who feeds
On the words, devouring them like bitter crumbs
That fill the stomach but will not germinate.
The devil is infertile, his heart is hard,
He gets no benefit from the words he eats,
But he knows Scripture; he has to keep on guard
Against Christ taking root in his victim's ears.
He gobbles it up, his bile breaks it down,
It turns to offal in his gut; he hears
Nothing turn to nothing that could be sound.
Like a worm turning books to excrement,
Leaving trails of holy evidence.

Mark 4:3–9; Psalm 119:105–112; Romans 11:8–10

75

PARABLE OF THE ROCKY GROUND

Some of the seeds fell on rocky ground.
Immediately, they took root and grew.
The roots could not go deep enough; they found
No water and wilted in the sun, the dew
Vanished in the noonday heat, the plumage died
Like stubble in a mown field. We know this well.
The rain falls, the wind blows, the pollen flies,
The spirit washes over us, we smell
Blooms in the desert, the flowers flourish, then drought
Parches the wastes, the stems dry up, turn red.
All of the hope a carpet of blossoms brought
Has perished in the heat and now is dead.
A parable that tells us all we know:
Only in rich, good soil can seedlings grow.

Luke 8:5–8; Isaiah 55:10–11; James 1:9–11

76

PARABLE OF THE THORNS
AND THISTLES

Among the thistles and thorns, he cast more seeds.
They grew, but the small shoots were crowded out.
In old gardens, trying to uproot the weeds,
We understand what this is all about:
Underneath the riot of growth, a leaf
Tries to break through a tangle toward the sun.
The rich growth of brambles in the turf
Will keep the farmer's work from getting done;
They smother the fragile plant until it dies,
Luxurious greenery that overwhelms
The new grown blossom gardeners tend to prize,
Rotting in the dirt, down in the devil's realm.
He leaves the decadent overgrowth to choke
The tiny leaflet and lets it go for broke.

Luke 8:5–8; 1 Timothy 6:9; 2 Timothy 4:10

77

PARABLE OF THE GOOD SOIL

The good soil: those who hear and understand,
Who let the words settle in and take root.
The soil oozes with waters feeding the plant.
After tending, it will bear much fruit.
A hundred, sixty, thirty times the yield
Of the tiny seed the sower cast about.
The reapers marvel at the fertile fields.
The crop ripens and sends its fruitage out
Into surprising places to do some good.
Planting its increase in a fallow place,
We'll watch it turn into Eucharists of food.
Bushels of good works from a present grace,
Filling and running over with much more
Than barns or granaries can ever store.

Matthew 13:3–9; Genesis 26:12–16; Colossians 2:6–7

78

THE GROWING SEED

The farmer goes out to his fields to see
The progress of his crop. He planted it
Some days ago. The rains have come; the seed
Is lying in the dirt. There's not a whit
He can do but wait. He sticks a thumb
Into the row to read the miracle,
Whether it germinated, when it will come
Out of its shell. Earth rings his fingernail
With fertile loam; he finds a tiny sprout
Small as a hair unwinding through the dark
While he slept. Soon, the black fields stretching out
Will green up; the growth and changing colors mark
Time's passing. He tilled the soil; now fields
Of gold ripple in the wind, heavy with yield.

Mark 4:26–29; Ecclesiastes 11:6; James 5:7

79

PARABLE OF THE SOWER EXPLAINED

He spoke in parables they did not understand.
They needed a key to explain every page
Of meanings. The reapers, angels, the Son of Man
Sends them to gather all at the end of the age.
Sinners and lawbreakers will be cast in the fire,
And then there will be weeping and gnashing of teeth.
The results of disobedience are dire.
Are we like Lear raging on the barren heath,
Furious mere mortals cannot divine their ends?
God knows who perishes and who is saved.
Choose now, be faithful to the One he sent:
Spurning the darker way of the depraved
To walk with Jesus deep into the light
Shining like the sun, each day more bright!

Matthew 13:13–17; Isaiah 6:9–10; Proverbs 4:18

80

THE WHEAT AND THE TARES

Innocent sleep after a hard day's work
Sowing the fields and then an enemy
Sneaks onto your farm in the dark; he lurks
Where you cannot see him, casting his seed
Far and wide. Their roots tangle in the soil
With the wheat, weaker rooted than the tares.
He plots to choke out the good seed and spoil
The harvest. He wants chaos and despair.
Let them be; as they sprout in the rich black loam,
Leave them to grow together, the Master says,
Weeding will tear up the good. The devil can roam
Sowing destruction in all his works and ways.
In the end, his produce will be gathered up
And thrown in a fire to perish without hope.

Matthew 13:24–30; 1 Corinthians 4:5; 1 Peter 5:6–11

81

PARABLE OF THE MUSTARD SEED

The smallest seed becomes the largest plant
In the garden. One for the books but workaday.
A girl from a backwater in a little land
Hears an angel. She wonders what to say—
Then assents. A lily shudders. A dove descends.
Beyond our grasp, the consequence breaks through.
The egg in her womb grows. It will have no end.
Its provenance unlikely, strange, but true.
A boy is born in a stable. The family moves
To Nazareth; he learns his Father's trade,
Healing the sick and hated for his love.
He is crucified—died and buried—then raised.
From the dead, he ascends. Now all the books in all
The world cannot contain him. They are too small.

Matthew 13:31–32; John 21:25; 2 Peter 3:18

82

THE LEAVEN IN THE LOAF

A woman empties a package of powdered yeast
Into three bushels of liquid, sugar, and flour,
And overnight it grows enough to feed
Hundreds. Fermentation gives it power.
It bubbles through the dough; we see it rise
And punch it down a couple times, then wait.
The mixture fills with air, quadrupling in size.
An ordinary mystery on our dinner plate.
It works through the meal utterly changing it.
He spoke a word in a close and airless room.
It went from one to another, it split and split.
Budding into air, a kingdom bloomed.
The mold broke into something we did not know—
Like seeing colors spin open, light explode.

Matthew 13:33; 1 Corinthians 5:6; Philemon 1:20

83

PARABLE OF THE TREASURE
IN THE FIELD

A man stumbled across a hidden treasure
In a field. He wanted it with all his might.
He covered it over and quickly took its measure
To buy the acreage. To his delight,
If he gathered everything he owned
And sold it for cash, he could redeem his joy.
He had just enough without a loan.
Spending himself poor did not destroy
His pleasure. It was everything to him.
When Saint Francis, heir to great wealth, desired
Lady Poverty, he gave everything
To court her. She set his very soul on fire.
He spent his birthright, all he could afford
To serve his lady and her ample Lord.

Matthew 13:44; Isaiah 55:1–2; Proverbs 2:1–5

84

PARABLE OF THE PEARL
OF GREAT PRICE

A merchant found a pearl of great price,
Which shone with a depth he had not seen before.
He wanted it, no matter the sacrifice;
To get it, he gladly would spend himself poor
For one precious jewel he had found.
Nothing had ever gladdened him so much.
His joy in owning it knew no bounds.
Contemplating it, he softly touched
Its iridescence, loving how light played
On its surface, like the portals of heaven
Shining of one great pearl. Its lusters made
All else dull. No offer could be given
To take it from him. The kingdom is the pearl
For which the martyrs died to save this world.

Matthew 13:45; Proverbs 2:1–5; Revelation 21:15–21

85

DRAWING IN THE NET

The net trawling the waters will gather up
Every kind of flotsam in the sea,
Fish to eat fresh, some to salt in a tub,
Others to cast away. The net would be
The kingdom, throwing its nets wide to catch
All that it can, every kind of fish.
Then see the judgment come; the angels watch
As they sort the rebels, those who do not wish
Renovation, who want to stay themselves.
Praying their will be done and not the Lord's,
Now discarded like the one of twelve
Who flung his silver on the temple floor,
Peering down the glimmering halls of hell,
Reckoning figures he could never tell.

Matthew 13:47–50; Matthew 25:31–33; John 21:11

86

THE NEW AND OLD TREASURES

To study Scripture, to open it up to others,
The scholars ransack both the new and old,
Searching their attics to unlock what they've discovered.
They feed on the Gospels, Jesus' story, and hold
Their master precious, they study to know him well.
They search thesauruses of prophecies
To find out who he is. They hear him tell
The multitudes by the azure seas
That he lives in Moses's or David's place,
Lawgiver and king, the prophesied.
Descending into the fires we could not face,
He harrows hell to preach to those who've died,
To bring out of death's regions a better word,
Unsealing the treasury, the key to all we've heard.

Matthew 13:51–52; Song of Songs 7:13; 1 Peter 4:6

87

JESUS' MOTHER AND BROTHERS

Who does he think he is? Where did he learn
All he is teaching us, wisdom beyond
Anything we have heard before. He turns
Everything upside down. He is the son
Of Joseph and Mary; we know his sisters and brothers.
How can he stand in the synagogue teaching,
Acting like Solomon? Just think of his mother.
She must blush when she hears her firstborn preaching.
No one understands what he says,
Telling us parables upending what we know.
Going against the nature of our ways.
A prophet among us, the Spirit's wind blows
Where it will. The Son of God comes down
To bring the heavens to our familiar rounds.

Mark 6:1–6; Isaiah 57:1–2; Hebrews 3:19

88

JESUS CHOOSES THE TWELVE

Out of the crush of followers, he called the Twelve—
One for each tribe of Israel—the first,
Andrew, then Simon Peter: to himself,
James and John, named Sons of Thunder, and third,
Philip and Bartholomew, and then
Matthew, Thomas, Thaddeus, and James the Less,
Simon and Judas (not the best of men).
Then he ordained them, gave them power, and blessed
Each apostle, sending them forth to preach
And cast out demons. The crowds grew and grew;
His family frightened, thought he should be seized.
He seemed out of his mind, what could they do?
He was their flesh, a brother under the skin,
Possessed with a spirit they did not reckon as kin.

Mark 3:13–21; Luke 6:14–16; 2 Corinthians 5:14

Sermon on the Mount

89

BEATITUDES

To bless, to say, blessed are you, to speak
A word rooted in sacrificial blood,
Jesus, the Torah in flesh, begins to preach
By blessing them; he teaches what is good
While the poor and hungry look for sustenance.
The words wash over them like fragrant balm.
Their lesions heal. They want to hear it again,
Its oil running down their faces, like a psalm
Whose words have run through their minds for years.
They dress a festering open wound with bliss,
Blessings like rain burbling in fields. We hear
Words washing over us. Words that can bless
The lacerations we have borne in pain
Now made level, the rough places plain.

Matthew 5:1; Genesis 27:30–38; Psalm 119:1–3

90

FIRST BEATITUDE

"Blessed are the poor in spirit, for theirs
Is the kingdom of heaven." Into their emptiness,
The Father pours out all his golden shares—
A heritage of good things, nothing less
Than dinner for my body and my soul.
When I am hungry, I receive his word;
It's more nutritious than a bar of gold.
There's life in death from gospels I have heard.
To leave this treasure, Jesus had to die.
They read his will; I hear he has arranged
To leave me all his goods, eternity,
Packed in a little crumb. In this exchange,
Christ makes me rich in bonds that last forever,
A wealth of blessings in a yard of heaven.

Matthew 5:3; Isaiah 61:1; Psalm 1:1–2

91

SECOND BEATITUDE

Jesus said, "Blessed are they who mourn;
They shall be comforted." To be sad,
Melancholy, anguished, all can be born
Of tragedy, from good things going bad,
To all the suffering we see everywhere.
Sorrow withers delight in family and friends,
We mumble hurts, sighing in constant prayer,
"Console us, Lord, as we face mortal ends."
As devastation looms, echoes of psalms
Tell us the Father hears and works to bring
Peace to our broken hearts; our spirits to calm.
In the midst of sadness, we can sing
Glad hallelujahs from the heart of grief,
God's mercies like summer rain drenching the leaves.

Matthew 5:4; 2 Corinthians 1:7; Revelation 7:11–17

92

THIRD BEATITUDE

"Blessed are the meek, for they shall inherit
The earth." Realtors cannot be meek.
They haggle over prices, rate the merit
Of properties, and outbid the weak.
But Jesus shows another truth to us.
In the end, the meek, waiting their turn,
Will prosper, quietly, without a fuss.
Heaven will descend, and we will learn
Who has purchase in the new creation.
The primogeniture of paradise
Is not by blood, or wealth, but our relation
To Adam's younger brother, Jesus Christ,
Whose garden he will make a heaven on earth,
A trust by virtue of our second birth.

Matthew 5:5; Psalm 37:11; Romans 4:13

93

ғоᴜʀᴛʜ ʙᴇᴀᴛɪᴛᴜᴅᴇ

He said, "Blessed are those who hunger and thirst
After righteousness, for they will be satisfied."
Water and food we need. They are first,
But more, those who have an appetite
For doing right are justified to help
Their neighbors flourish, knowing Christ has done
Everything so we can do things well,
So justice runs down like waters in the sun.
Without this satisfaction, we can fail,
Lose pleasure in the task of making things
Function so they work and good prevails.
Jesus will feed us so our spirit sings.
He came to give us everything we need,
To sanctify our thoughts and words and deeds.

Matthew 5:6; Isaiah 55:1–2; Micah 6:8

94

FIFTH BEATITUDE

"Blessed are the merciful, for they
Shall receive mercy." The merciful
Empty themselves for others every day,
Struggle against evil, all that is cruel.
They show kindness, wipe away the tears
Of sorrow from the face of those who weep
For solace. They nurse the sick, calm the fears
Of those whose nightmares terrorize their sleep,
But what they spend is always recompensed.
Our God pours balm into their weary hearts;
There is no emptiness so vast, immense
God cannot fill with mercies, not one part.
They revel in the richness they receive
For all the consolations that they give.

Matthew 5:7; Proverbs 19:17; James 2:13

95

SIXTH BEATITUDE

"Blessed are the pure in heart, for they
Shall see God." How can a heart be pure?
Pollution in rivers we filter away
So we can drink from fountains clean and clear.
The human heart is vain and filled with rot.
Nothing I do can wash up its messes.
I am not pure of heart. Will I see God?
There are such folks, and them he blesses.
He sees them shining around him. It baffles me.
On my own terms, I want to see my Lord,
Not as he says, in others, I want to see
His face, to worship him forevermore,
The font of crystal waters that I crave—
It's my impurities I want to save.[1]

Matthew 5:8; Psalm 24:3–4; Hebrews 12:14

---

[1] Published in *Christian Century* 136, no. 22 (October 2019): https://tinyurl.com/y4dw79w7.

96

SEVENTH BEATITUDE

"Blessed are the peacemakers, for they
Shall be called children of God." To make peace
Means more than stopping the fight, ending the fray,
Harder than declaring wars should cease.
Something must be changed, a rift be healed,
So life is wholesome and all things work together
For good to flourish in the commonweal,
Hard labor to assure that all are treasured.
For this, they shall be called children of God.
Are not all of us, each one, a child
Of God? In baptism, it's what we're called.
Like squaring the circle, how do we reconcile
That outsiders are numbered as his own;
How are we inside troublemakers known?

Matthew 5:9; James 3:18; Romans 8:14

97

EIGHTH BEATITUDE

"Blessed are those who are persecuted
For righteousness' sake, theirs is the kingdom of heaven."
He blesses those whose witness cannot be muted,
Who defend the truths that Jesus gives them.
They suffer agony for what is right
And never flinch. The world strikes out in hate,
Preferring darkness to the morning light.
They have to quench it; on and on they prate
Against the innocents who do what's good.
They try to ruin a realm they cannot stand,
A heritage the martyrs understood:
A glimpse of glory in a grain of sand.
They suffer paradise in all they do;
It glimmers in their vision, lovely, true.

Matthew 5:10; 2 Timothy 2:12; 1 Peter 3:14–16

98

SALT OF THE EARTH

"You are the salt of the earth; if you have lost
The saltiness I make of all of you,
What use will you be? Better to be tossed
Out on the street and be trodden underfoot."
Salt is necessary: it preserves,
It even heals, but too much of it kills.
A dash enhances taste in the food we serve,
Controls the plasma flowing, keeps us well.
Our work is to be salty, change the world
By adding flavor to our daily mess
So others, bored as any teenaged girl
Doing her nails and primping, want no less
Than Jesus' blessing to make them worth their salt
And bring a seasoned finish to their faults.

Matthew 5:13; Colossians 4:5–6; 1 Peter 3:15–17

99

JESUS, THE LIGHT OF THE WORLD

Because he is the light, we are light,
Meant to shine like a city on a hill
For all to see, a beacon in the night
Showing through the darkness the Father's will
So pilgrims can be guided to the truth
As the darkest shadows in the house are cleared,
Casting out the demons crouched in the room,
Filling the space with Christ who has appeared
So others can lounge in his brilliance and live
Free of the devil lurking in the dark;
His furtive mission to destroy what we believe
Dying in sunlight. We are to make our mark
In the world, lighting the way we have been given:
Jesus, come down in flesh to bring us heaven.

Matthew 5:14–16; Ephesians 5:8–21; Philemon 1:6

100

JESUS EXPOUNDING THE LAW

Hard words. Hard as bright gems. He is the Law
And came not to abolish it but keep
It, to fulfill it; he knows the lines, our flaws.
After blessings we reckoned on the cheap,
He lets the hammer fall. Not a mite
Can be interpreted away or shirked.
They shine like diamonds, their facets always bright.
We turn them over, grace sparkles into works.
Casuists, Matthew catches us at our game:
Trying to weasel out of Sinai's commands,
To prove them fool's gold, repudiate the blame
For our rebellion from all that Christ demands.
Like fudging on our taxes, making up rules
That save us from declaring the family jewels.

Matthew 5:17–20; Romans 3:31; James 2:10–13

101

ANGER

Murder is sin, the worst, Jesus says,
But digs deeper. Anger begets hate.
Its caustic fumes embitter and infect
Everything unless its smoky fires abate.
Our rage, like smog, chokes us, the air we breathe;
Nothing can escape its acrid smell.
It turns us away from loved ones; our spirits seethe,
Their banked embers kindle a living hell.
It cuts us off. Haters live alone,
Bitter and tiresome to their only friends.
This law is made for us to flourish; the one
Who makes it knows us and has better ends
For us than smoldering in a fog of wrath.
He sees its costs, its deadly aftermath.

Matthew 5:21–26; Deuteronomy 5:17; Ephesians 4:25–27

102

CONFESSION AND FORGIVENESS

Hatred, resentment, and spite poison the soul.
Say you are sorry, even if you are right!
Jesus' sermon gives us no loophole.
He sees the gaping wounds in these blights
To love. Their consequences he knows well,
So he requires we reconcile before
We worship, before our sin bears fruit and hell
Opens its maw, dropping us through the floor
Into chaos. Back in the day, people knew
The rules. Before communion, they would speak
With their pastor, confess their sins, and do
As Jesus said: big strong farmers would weep
And settle with their neighbor face-to-face
Before they drank proof of their Savior's grace.

Matthew 5:21–26; Exodus 20:13; Ephesians 4:25–27

103

LUST

Even to look at someone with lustful intent
Is adulterous, Jesus says. A single man
Without sin, he knew what the commandment meant.
Women loved and followed him. They ran
After him, in love with him because
He took them as they were, wounded and hurt
By urges needful and set in nature's laws
For the world to flourish. God shaped out of earth
Adam and Eve, whose hymeneal song
Echoes through wedding music—at last, at last,
Bone of my bone, flesh of my flesh, they longed
For each other, the child an emblem of their past.
This force exists for purposes we know
Are good but when ungoverned, oh what woe.

Matthew 5:27–30; 2 Samuel 11:1–5; 2 Peter 2:18–20

104

ADULTERY

A body knows the faith that it defiles
When it trespasses on sacred oaths.
Betrayals, secrets, evasions, and cold denials
Unmask our nakedness and make us both
Lose the innocence of knowing trust;
Not seeing what deceit easily reveals,
This is the evil of untrammeled lust.
The hurts make scars that never can be healed.
We retreat to our inner parts alone,
See other shades dance in our lover's eyes.
Guilt and shame gather around with stones
Ready to pummel us for all our lies.
Enter the kingdom of heaven less a hand
Than use it to fire up what lust demands.

Matthew 5:27–30; Proverbs 6:27–29; 2 Peter 2:14

105

DIVORCE

Why does he talk about divorce that way,
Leaving not a speck of wiggle room?
We misconstrue all he meant to say,
Trying to get off and escape our doom.
There's sorrow here, for what he says is right.
One cannot blot away what one has done,
For everything hidden will come to light.
If we betray and love another one,
A touch forbidden by an oath we swore
Cannot be unremembered nor overlooked,
For we are wed to all we've done before.
Forgiven, yes, but written in the book.
A paper cannot nullify our past,
Deeds are not undone; they last and last.

Matthew 5:31–32; Deuteronomy 24:1–4; Malachi 2:13–16

106

FALSE OATHS

Christ says believers should tell the truth.
A lie corrupts the social fabric, tears
Apart our bonds, expecting the law's sharp tooth
To keep the faith when villains calmly swear
On stacks of Bibles, knowing they are false.
When we take the name of God in vain,
We increase the gravity of our faults.
Blasphemy. Prevarication stains
What's worthy. One lie begets another lie.
Most liars' oaths, untrue, are lightly taken;
They are convicts of their perjury.
They'll soon be caught in a mesh of their own making.
Better for all when yes means yes and no
Means no. It saves our commonwealth from woe.

Matthew 5:33–36; Deuteronomy 23:21–23; James 5:12

107

VENGEANCE

Getting even—we say revenge is sweet—
That contradicts what Jesus has to say.
Telling us we should turn the other cheek,
To act in kindness, to show a better way.
His rule of law turns everything around.
Surprise with mercy the one who leaves you hurt.
It changes the energy. Stand your ground.
Your foes expect that you will do them dirt
Or smash their faces. This puts them off balance, fakes
Them out. Pausing, they'll wonder what comes next.
A way to stop evil in its tracks.
We've memorized the script, an ancient text,
The pas de deux, a dance we know by heart.
Jesus instructs us: play a different part.

Matthew 5:38–42; Proverbs 20:22; Romans 12:19–21

108

LOVE YOUR ENEMIES

Love our enemies? This is too hard!
What does Jesus mean? Love those we hate!
Act kindly toward them? Can I change my heart?
Doing good for evil could unlock a gate.
He does not say, "Approve their evil deeds,
All that they do to bring destruction"—no!
Love them! Think of their human wants and needs,
Pray for them, serve them, change their status quo.
God's mercies show us best what we might do,
Sending the rain and sunshine down on all,
Evil and good receive the same; it's true.
So all the living can flourish, the great, the small.
Loving deeds might change our foe to friend.
Who knows where small conversions have their end?

Matthew 5:43–48; Psalm 7:3–5; 1 John 4:20–21

109

DISCOURSE ON OSTENTATION [A]

If we give money so we can win great praise,
The alms will help the poor, but our reward
Will die like silver dew on a summer day.
Practice charity in secret, says our Lord.
Your Father in heaven will see it and be glad.
To please the Lord with works, how can this be?
We know God's righteousness cannot be had
By our own efforts. The grace of God is free.
The secret hidden in this word is rich.
A heart that treasures mercy, its great wealth,
Takes pleasure helping someone in the ditch,
Quietly restoring the wounded to health.
We know our Father watches this with joy,
With compliments of blessings, pure, unalloyed.

Matthew 6:1–1; Obadiah 1:3–4; 1 Corinthians 13:3

110

DISCOURSE ON OSTENTATION [B]

Heroes of prayer, people who spend hours
Storming the gate of heaven should take care
Showing others how they access godly powers.
Prayer should be private, not having trumpets blare
As we take our place before others to pray.
We listen to ourselves. God knows our wants.
A quick breathed sigh of thanks, requests that state
Our needs. Keep the lines open, never flaunt
The time. Do it in secret. Old cronies talk
Forever and never weary of the time.
Their banter rambles like a Sunday walk.
Suddenly, the trivial turns sublime,
Checking in often, cherishing our friend,
Staying in touch, always, world without end.

Matthew 6:2–4; 2 Kings 4:33; 1 Thessalonians 5:16–18

The Lord's Prayer

111

INTRODUCTION

Our Father, Jesus says, and gives us ties
That bind: one to him, who lives in heaven,
And others who learn to say his name with sighs,
Dying for a Father who loves and wants to give them
All good things, to hold them in his arms,
Keeping them from danger when they are young,
Raising them to stand bravely against harm
When threatened by dissension, chaos, or wrong,
To face with confidence the evil days.
The devil and his empty promises
Scatter before us; all his works and ways
We must renounce. God fosters all of us,
A sire who fashions us to be like him.
His image shines in us; it cannot dim.

Matthew 6:9–13; Psalm 33:13–15; Colossians 3:9–10

112

FIRST PETITION /
HALLOWED BE THY NAME

We pray to the holy God above, be God,
Make your name hallowed, sanctify yourself.
We fall before you, quaking with love and awe.
Your presence fills us with reverence, overwhelms
Our paltry monuments, soon frivolous dust
Eroding in the wind to nameless sand.
You are the only God we dare to trust,
To reach toward when our idol's marble hand
Is broken chips. To the holy, we kneel down,
Feeling in our flesh we are not equal to
This sanctity that trembles the solid ground,
Rocking us to worship. Nothing will do
But God, whose word is sacred: hallowed be
Thy name, an old declension that bends the knee.

Matthew 6:9; Isaiah 29:23; Habakkuk 2:20

113

SECOND PETITION /
THY KINGDOM COME

Why do we pray "thy kingdom come" each day?
The words tumble out of our mouths like dreams.
We will see Jesus when he comes, we pray.
But is it only the end we see that gleams
At the brim of daylight? It comes when he is near,
When he walks into a room and says, "Repent!
The kingdom is at hand, my friends, right here!
I am the paradise my Father sends."
Having the Holy Spirit dwell in us
Brings eternity into our hearts of flesh.
It builds a temple in us, a spacious house,
A place to abide with us in every breath,
Showing us the lights of heaven break
Across the far horizon as we wake.

Matthew 6:10; Romans 14:17; 2 Timothy 4:1–3

114

THIRD PETITION / THY WILL BE DONE ON EARTH AS IT IS IN HEAVEN

To pray, "thy will be done on earth as in heaven,"
Is hard. Can I submit to God's left hand
Working against my will and all I'm given?
The heavenly forces gather at his command,
Ready to follow him through heaven and earth.
The great battalions of his angels fly
Invisibly through all the universe,
Guarding, protecting, doing his works, they ride,
Giving order to chaos. They get things done.
I cannot see them but believe they are there;
Even when evil seems to overcome
All that is good, he listens to my prayer.
But do I pray to live untouched myself,
Praying thy will be done for everyone else?

Matthew 6:10; Psalm 103:20–22; Hebrews 1:14

115

FOURTH PETITION / GIVE US THIS DAY OUR DAILY BREAD

"Give us this day our daily bread," we say—
Suddenly, we listen; this is about us!
The fourth petition turns to our flesh; we pray
For good health and daily sustenance,
Something we can set our teeth into.
We ask for rain and sunshine, golden fields.
God gives all, even the wicked, food,
Old friends, good government, all that yields
Contentment. We have a god who likes to give
Things that are tangible and down to earth,
All the necessities we need to live.
So we take our pleasures here for all they're worth.
Rich in abundance even without our thanks,
A wealth we cannot salt away in banks.

Matthew 6:11; Joel 2:22–27; Acts 14:15–17

116

FIFTH PETITION / FORGIVE US OUR TRESPASSES AS WE FORGIVE THOSE WHO TRESPASS AGAINST US

"Forgive us," we pray to God, and he forgives
Our trespasses when we step over a line,
A lawful boundary and, unthinking, grieve
Another. God absolves these debts of mine.
This I have been taught and understand,
A grace sufficient to cover the worst of sins.
Harder to give up a grudge, reach out a hand
Despite the hurt, be kind, begin again.
Not I'm sorry, but I forgive, like God,
Who's asking me to do what he has done,
Pardon my enemies for all their flaws.
Doing it because of his dear Son.
Like God, giving those who hurt me grace
Crosses a line into a holy space.

Matthew 6:12; 2 Corinthians 2:5–11; Ephesians 4:32

117

SIXTH PETITION / LEAD US NOT INTO TEMPTATION

Lord, lead us not into temptation, keep
Us from divisions where the tempter dwells.
My past is shriven, but I can fall asleep
And stray into the real estate of hell
By letting down my guard. Jesus went
Into the desert and found the devil there.
He fought the trickster to the bitter end,
Using his Father's word, Scripture, prayer.
Do not let us be tempted beyond our strength.
Our will falters against satanic powers.
We know that he will go to any length
To lure us where his noxious seeds will flower.
Lord, do not let him test me, come make me strong,
And lead me through the wastelands where Legion throngs.

Matthew 6:13; 1 Corinthians 10:13; 2 Timothy 4:17–18

118

SEVENTH PETITION /
DELIVER US FROM THE EVIL ONE

Deliver us, Lord, from the evil one
Who roams about seeking whom he may devour,
Snatch us up out of his grip. Be gone!
In Jesus' name, we whisper every hour.
Even in our orderly homes he is there
Waiting for any opportunity.
My aged parents prayed their evening prayers
Confident and firm in the belief
That God watched over them. They knew that death
Was crouching outside to unravel their estates,
Scatter their habits, take away their breath.
Innocent of their end, its final date,
They lay down sighing petitions they knew well,
Asking safe conduct over the shafts of hell.

Matthew 6:13; Psalm 4:8; 1 Peter 5:8–9

119

CONCLUSION / FOR THINE IS THE POWER AND THE GLORY, FOREVER AND EVER. AMEN

From the Father in the highest heaven
To the devil in the deep regions of hell,
The Lord's Prayer shows us all that we are given:
Geographies of mercy for ourselves
When Jesus gives us prayers we need to live,
A daily map of how we ought to pray.
He builds the mansions that his mercy gives,
The glory at the end of our pilgrim way.
There we'll enjoy him and the home he built,
Where all will be accomplished, all be known
Without a particle of shame or guilt.
Now we are safe; his Father is our own.
We dwell in gardens by a crystal stream.
Its cadence marks the measures of our dreams.

Matthew 6:9–13; John 14:1–4; Romans 8:26–27

120

THE BIRDS OF HEAVEN

See the birds of the air, swooping up and down,
Flitting from here to there, chirping sweet songs.
They are not anxious, good seed is all around,
But everything they do all day long
Is search for food. And usually they are fed.
We have to feed our children every day.
They look to us for milk and daily bread;
We know of those starving not so far away,
How can we not worry? Jesus shows
Fretting is useless knowing he will provide.
None of our fears can make potatoes grow.
All we can do is plant and wait. The birds glide
Over the trees, up and around their nests;
A flight of winter seeds feeds their requests.

Matthew 6:25–27; Job 38:41; Psalm 147:8–9

121

THE LILIES OF THE FIELD

The lilies of the field, they neither spin
Nor weave; not even Solomon was clothed
In such glory. The brilliant whites, like a dappled scrim
Waving in the sunlight, for his fashion show—
God dresses them in vibrant colors, rich
In fabrics the finest tailors could not design.
All for our pleasure, painting the humblest ditch,
Prodigal his palette, beauty his line.
Down the runway might prance another sorrow,
But worry will not stop it. It's how we live.
The rose and thorn will grow today, tomorrow;
Colorful buds will blossom, and God will give
More than we need, raiment for all our days;
Linger by their loveliness. Give praise.

Matthew 6:27–34; 1 Kings 10:4–9; Psalm 90:5–6

122

DISCOURSE ON JUDGING

We all preach against another's sins.
Seeing the mote in others, we do not see
The summons we are writing, not a hint,
Accuses us. We laugh critically,
Judging the judge, leaving ourselves outside
The courtroom, awaiting a verdict we've prepared.
Jesus says our case needs to be tried,
A litigation that must end in prayer.
Lord, cleanse our sight of all the splintered truths
That blind us to our flaws. Open our eyes,
Help us to see ourselves as others do,
To prosecute our errors and be surprised
By those whom we have roughly tried to help,
Whose faults lumber around within ourselves.

Matthew 7:1–5; 2 Samuel 12:1–15; Romans 2:1–11

123

DISCOURSE ON HOLINESS

Old tracts printed images of the two ways:
The broad way heads down, the narrow up
Into light eternal. We see the saints
Greeting with joy believers whose fervent hope
In the promises they cherished and believed
Brought them home. The broad way, like Vanity Fair,
Is populated with souls who take their ease
And perish. They catapult through the air
Into hell where every appetite is scored.
The straitened way to heaven is difficult
But the company peerless. We walk with our Lord,
Taking our pleasures, feeling the gaping gulf
Between heaven and earth is erased,
Eternity easing each step with grace.

Matthew 7:13–27; Psalm 16:11; Galatians 6:9–10

124

THE TEST OF A GOOD PERSON

Beware false prophets, our Lord Jesus says,
Who sound like they're connected, acting holy.
Dressed like sheep but wolves who know the ways
Saints act. They sigh and speak of God solely.
It takes a season for any graft to grow.
After a long time, we will come to see
Ripeness or rottenness and will know
The truth, whether the juice flowing in the tree
Bubbles from fresh waters. Knowing the talk,
Discerning the spirit, sends us into prayer
So we can trust our shepherd walks the walk
And will not lure us like a wolf into his lair.
We need to fathom the fruit he bears to tell
The libations he is quaffing from what well.

Matthew 7:15–20; Deuteronomy 13:1–5; Acts 13:4–12

125

THE WISE AND FOOLISH BUILDERS

If we're wise, we'll build our house on the rock.
Even though wild rains and floods will come
With gales battering the doors and walls,
They will not fall, and we will be at home.
For when we live trusting God's word is true,
We will be safe, the promise will stand fast
Against storms that cannot be subdued.
Unshakeable foundations, they last and last.
The foolish build their homes on shifting sand,
No bedrock there to keep them from flying away,
Lifted by tempests sweeping across the land,
Scattering into the clouds where the wind holds sway,
Flying like flotsam through the dingy air,
Shrieking for sounder footings, solid and square.

Matthew 7:24–29; Ezekiel 13:10–14; 1 Corinthians 3:10–15

Down from the Mountain

126

JESUS CLEANSES A LEPER

Down from the mountain, Jesus meets leprosy.
A man, unclean, wanting to be healed,
Not to be touched, he cries out to be seen.
The healer, at once, grabs him so he can feel
Skin against skin, wholeness against death.
He worships him there, kneeling before the Lord,
One he will serve as long as he has breath.
Ministering to this man's soul, but more—
Jesus knows illness concentrates
Our minds on the hurt, shrinking flesh and blood
To a wound that rules our body and our fate.
What we want is the lesion repaired, made good,
To go down to the square and plumb forget
That pain was all I knew until we met.

Matthew 8:1–4; Leviticus 14:2–31; 3 John 1:2–4

127

HEALING OF THE CENTURION'S SON

The Roman understood authority
And knew Jesus had it. The soldier would say,
"Go!" and his charges went. Jesus could speak
And the forces of the universe obeyed.
All the Gentile needed was a word,
One that would heal his son. Jesus paused
To marvel as he healed the boy; stirred
By such faith, he prophesied what he saw:
Joyful believers coming from east and west
To sit at the banquet feasting with Abraham,
Isaac, and Jacob, together with all the blest
Enjoying the party, the supper of the Lamb,
Together because they all believed in him,
Not the bloodlines of Jacob or Bethlehem.

Matthew 8:5–13; Isaiah 59:19; Revelation 22:1–5

128

RAISING THE YOUNG MAN FROM
NAIN FROM THE DEAD

A weeping mother, crowds of mourners, a corpse,
Portents of Jesus' fate looming ahead.
Her only son gone, bitter remorse
Wails in her throat; her hope and future dead.
Who will take care of her? Frantic with fear,
Afraid of what will come. He shares her grief—
"Do not weep," he says, going to the bier.
Touching the man's remains, they all believe
Makes Jesus unclean. Now he will have to wash
His own body of death to walk around.
"Young man, arise." The boy sits up and talks.
What does he say? Does his mother kneel down?
See, in their midst, all that is holy moves
Down from the heav'ns—death purged away by love.

Luke 7:11–17; 1 Kings 17:17–24; Haggai 2:13

129

MESSENGERS FROM JOHN THE BAPTIST TO CHRIST

John the Baptist, in prison looking out,
Wonders, after hearing of Christ's good deeds,
Was he the one, his confidence in doubt,
All he had suffered, now a broken reed.
Honey and locusts had been his hermit fare.
Brooding, he asked Jesus, had he been wrong.
Pointing to him, "Prepare the way, prepare!"
Badgered and beset, his wildness gone—
Jesus refined the question John had asked:
"Yes, these things are true, the prophets said,
'The blind will see, the deaf will hear, my task
Is bringing the kingdom of heaven near, the dead
Rise up, the poor are fed.' Blessed are you,
All your preaching in the desert has come true."

Matthew 11:2–18; Isaiah 35:5–7; James 2:5

130

THE VIOLENT BEAR IT AWAY

Jesus treasures peace; the only arms
He bore reached out to comfort human woe,
Healing the sick, doing good, not harm.
He panicked the demons. We fight the ancient foe
Who seeks to stop us, the one who crucifies
Innocence itself, who cuts off heads,
Martyrs the ones who see the tempter's lies,
Until all his followers are dead.
Why does this scapegoat make the old guard rage?
They turn their weapons against a man of peace,
Bearing him off into the darkest age.
Violent against a voice that will not cease;
They use all their artillery, whips, and guns
Trying to save the world from God's own Son.

Matthew 11:11–15; Psalm 2:1–3; Malachi 3:1–3

131

THE TWO DEBTORS AT SIMON'S HOME

A flask of alabaster, clothes torn and soiled.
A woman of the city washes his feet
With her tears, anointing him with fragrant oil,
Spending her poverty from the wanton street.
Jesus knew her, all that she had done.
With him, she felt forgiven, clean, and whole.
They all looked down at her; most everyone
In the place had known her. He reached into her soul
And healed her. "Her sin was great," poor Simon thought,
"I have been righteous, kept the covenant.
I owe nothing, wanting what she has got.
My being covets all the good she's spent.
He's lavish with his mercy for a whore,
No little room for her within his store."

Luke 7:36–50; Genesis 18:4; 1 Timothy 1:12–14

132

WEALTHY WOMEN SERVE JESUS

"Foxes have holes, and birds of the air have nests,
But the Son of Man has no place to lay his head,"
Jesus observed. Wealthy women, Luke says,
Ministered to him, grateful for all he said.
A man who healed their wounds and made them whole,
Like Mary Magdalene, whom he had freed
Of seven demons. She loved him heart and soul
For all he did and said, happy to feed
His hungry body with food her hands prepared,
Washing his clothes, keeping his wardrobe clean,
Darning his robes when the thorns would cut and tear
The fabric. Not much mentioned, barely seen,
Homemaking for him, sisters in the word,
Rich in conversation, treasures heard.

Luke 8:1–3; Matthew 27:55–56; Luke 24:10–11

133

STUDENTS ARE LIKE THEIR TEACHERS

These truths unsettle us. To follow him
Makes us like him, he says; we're not above
Our teacher, we experience his fate. It's grim:
Rejected, beaten, crucified for love.
Must we bear the world's hatred as he
Because we're his? O Lord, we are not strong
Enough to walk alone to Calvary.
We hear your warnings and know they are not wrong.
To speak for you brings suffering all its own,
The wounds of faith. Satan's party hates
The thought of your ruling from heaven's throne.
It drives them to furies of chaos they create.
To be like you is life at the very heart.
The benefits are glory, the way is hard.

Matthew 10:24–25; 2 Corinthians 4:1–12; Hebrews 12:3

134

SHEEP AMONG WOLVES

If you are a lamb among wolves, be wise
As serpents and as innocent as doves,
A menagerie of deadly enemies.
Sheep are stupid; they panic, push, and shove,
Making them vulnerable. Jesus sends
His lambs, the ones he shepherds, into the fray.
Is this how Jesus wants to be our friend?
To make us suffer hatred as easy prey;
Where evil men will haul us into court,
Accusing us of every sort of crime?
Our Father will speak through us to their reports.
To follow Christ is dying all the time,
Yet he leads us into life beyond mere death,
The end of every rapture known to flesh.

Matthew 10:16; Romans 16:19; Philippians 2:14–18

135

COMMISSIONING THE
TWELVE APOSTLES

Jesus sends the twelve apostles out to be
His body in the world, to share his love,
Compassion for the sorrow that he sees:
To touch the poor, the ailing, to put salve
On the wounds of those we serve for his dear sake.
Our duty is to pray that he will send
Workers to get his mission done, to take
Nothing; all that we need he gives to mend
The broken. The Adoniram Judsons believed
What Jesus is saying here. They heard his call
And ended up in Burma. Ann received
Courage to suffer and die, in her love for all,
Fighting child marriage, the killing of baby girls:
The tears of Christ sending her into the world.

Matthew 10:1–15; 1 Chronicles 12:18; Psalm 119:176

136

NOTHING IS HIDDEN

Fear not; one day all will be revealed,
And what is done in darkness will be known,
Shouted from the rooftops. They can kill
The body; beware of those who kill the soul.
Fear not; your Father watches over you.
He numbers each hair that falls to the ground.
All you can do for him is tell the truth
So one day at the end, you will be found
Ready for heaven. For now, it will be rough.
They will hate the way you honor me
By speaking my name in public. It is enough
To hear your witness out in the thronging street.
Then I will testify I heard your cry
Naming my name, a truth I won't deny.

Matthew 10:26–33; Isaiah 51:5–7; Revelation 22:16–17

137

NOT PEACE BUT A SWORD

"I came not to bring peace but a sword."
This goes against the gospel many preach,
"Peace, peace," they say, missing his cutting word.
A blade divides, a necessary breach
Shearing us from the past when we hear his call
To tell others we have met the one
Who long ago was promised, after the fall,
To heal the rift. It is God's only Son
Able to slice the scab of blood away
And give us something more. Instead of kin,
A fellowship with him our heart obeys.
A father or a mother cannot win
Our love while hating us for our beliefs;
He cuts us from old bonds, a relative grief.

Luke 12:49–53; Micah 7:5–7; 2 Corinthians 5:14–15

138

BEHEADING OF JOHN THE BAPTIST

Herod, captive to his lusts, killed John
For railing against his adulteries.
Made wanton by a dance, he swore upon
His honor to give the dancer what she pleased.
Her mother prompted her to work revenge,
"Request the head of John upon a dish."
The rottenness of Herod made a stench;
Keeping his lurid oath for a tantrum wish
Afraid of John, knowing he spoke the truth,
He ordered him beheaded, the head brought
To Salome, steeped in blood from her youth.
We never hear what her cruel mother thought.
Grisly, wanting his death, the severed head
On a plate, the appetite to see him dead.

Matthew 14:1–12; Genesis 40:20–22; Leviticus 18:16–21

139

fEEDING THE fIVE THOUSAND

All he craved after the boat ride was rest.
Hungering to be alone, away from the crowds,
And grief for his cousin John, weariness
Overcame him; still they followed from the towns.
They needed him like food, to heal their sick,
To cast out demons, ravenous to be whole.
This man of flesh, touching them to the quick.
He was paradise, a living scroll
Like prophets munched on, honey to their tongues,
Calligraphy for bread. He gave thanks
And broke five loaves, two fish, they passed among
Thousands, sating all the famished ranks,
Victuals enough to feed the boys and girls,
And women tasting the chewy miracle.

Matthew 14:13–21; 2 Kings 4:42–44; Ezekiel 3:1–3

140

JESUS WALKS ON THE WATER

After his prayers, he strides the rolling waves,
The winds whaling into his flesh and bone,
A tabernacle, the great I AM, a nave
Riding the darkness, light as a skipping stone.
The disciples seeing him on the water shriek
In terror, thinking they have seen a ghost.
"Take heart, it is I," the Savior speaks,
"Be not afraid!" They see him now up close.
Peter, wanting to show his faith, cries out,
"Command me to come!" leaping toward him in hope,
But the howling winds swamp him in his doubt.
"Lord, save me!" he screams. The Lord lifts him up,
"Where is your faith?" snatching him out of the storm
As the fierce winds cease, scaring them even more.

Matthew 14:22–33; Deuteronomy 31:6; Isaiah 41:13

141

HEALING IN GENNESARET

They knew him, bringing their sick from everywhere,
Pallets and cots lying around him, running to find
The ill, everyone for whom they cared
Who needed healing: the halt, the deaf, the blind.
He drew them to him; they knew that he could heal,
Even a fringe of his garment was enough.
Belief ran through them like a fever; they could feel
His medicine flood through them with a touch.
Grasping at his worn and homespun sleeve,
All of the remedies in the world flowed out of him,
The Great Physician; all of them believed
He could make them well, restoring them,
Bodies and spirits as whole and innocent
As the first good day they had ever spent.

Mark 6:45–56; Psalm 6:2; Acts 5:14–16

The Bread of Life Discourses

142

I AM THE BREAD OF LIFE [A]

I am the manna in the wilderness,
The bread my Father sent so you could live.
But I am living bread and nothing less;
Ambrosian treats only a god can give.
With manna, you survived and did not die
For lack of food, but read the desert wastes
To find sandy places where old bones lie.
I am the bread that flesh and spirit taste.
These are the delicacies I serve to feed
Mortals, a food that's more than bread alone.
All you desire, more than a body needs,
You will become perfected flesh and bone
Raised up and resurrected, something new,
A wonder in the grain I give to you.

John 6:22–59; Exodus 16:6–35; Nehemiah 9:13–15

143

I AM THE BREAD OF LIFE [B]

Imagine! A man, flesh and blood, who makes
Baskets of food for thousands says he is bread.
Divinity to chew on, loaves he bakes
On the mountainside where everyone is fed.
Mixed with metaphor, the means to live,
All of life comes down from heav'n in his flesh.
His words the sustenance his body gives
So every day we see things new and fresh.
But deeper still, all things proceed from him.
It's not just physical; it's even more:
This man from heav'n whose light will never dim
Will feed us paradise from his rich store
So we can revel in our second birth,
Feasting on eternity bred for earth.

John 6:22–34; Psalm 78:23–24; 1 Corinthians 10:1–5

144

YOU WILL NEVER DIE

If this means, like Tithonus,[2] I will age
Forever, a head on a pillow, no thanks.
Death is the enemy, an empty page,
But Jesus knows what I do not. He drank
The cup and perished on an awful tree,
Went to the dead, and on the third day rose,
Fully alive, something the twelve could see
But not quite fathom; his risen body showed
A radiance language cannot describe.
We'll be translated into wholeness, another realm,
Knit back into the truth, the laws of scribes
Vanished into light, overwhelmed,
The senses cleansed to hear the noonday sun,
See music out of time, and death undone.

John 6:41–51; 1 Corinthians 15:35–49; 1 Peter 1:3–9

---

[2] A Greek myth in which Tithonus, a mortal, was granted eternal life but not eternal youth by Zeus.

145

EAT MY FLESH

His word makes bread his body, wine his blood
So we can take his flesh into our own.
Its substance grows in us like any food
So Christ becomes our flesh and bone.
Eternity inhabits all our breath.
We live even after our hearts have quit
Because our Savior has defeated death.
We feed on immortality to fit
Ourselves for heaven, fare his word imparts.
We trust the promise Jesus Christ is near.
Chemists can do their tests, study the heart,
And see nothing happening, nothing here.
But in this crumb of bread and sip of wine,
I will be made, despite myself, divine.

John 6:52–59; 1 John 4:12–13; Revelation 1:17–18

146

THE WORDS OF ETERNAL LIFE

To eat the Master's flesh—a stumbling block—
It scandalized them; to hear it made them sick.
On top of that claiming he was a god!
Many left; they could not stomach him.
The hocus pocus they think Jesus used
Makes unbelievers crazy. What does he mean,
To chew on God's body, against all taboos?
He is like nobody we have ever seen:
Miraculous, he speaks in metaphors,
Figures of speech like similes and signs.
We take them on one level, nothing more,
But his sayings upend the flatlands of our minds.
We want the faith to understand his words.
And flee the auguries we fear we've heard.

John 6:60–66; Jeremiah 17:1; 2 Corinthians 3:3–11

147

PETER'S REPLY

Down from the mountain, Peter saw the light.
Jesus' sermon cleansed his unbelief,
And finally, the eager vicar got it right
After many mistakes that gave him grief.
He hungered after Jesus' holy word.
No one else brought life into his flesh
That raised him up; no one he had heard
Spoke truth that satisfied him and refreshed
His being. No philosopher who tried
To change his mind had ever changed his heart.
Here stood the truth incarnate at his side,
The very God of gods to light the dark.
Christ's waters quenched his dry and thirsty soul;
His body and his blood had made him whole.

John 6:66–69; Acts 5:20; 1 John 4:16

148

JUDAS

The heart of darkness lurked in their midst,
Waiting the moment to hand over God's Son
To the mercies of his enemies with a kiss!
The silver in his bags, the deed will be done.
Judas hated the Lord he once obeyed
For not being bloodthirsty enough.
It was Jesus, he figured, who had betrayed
His cause. Spiritual food could not do much
To topple the oppressive Roman guard,
Drive them out, send them back to Rome.
He watched her laving Christ's body with costly nard,
Anointing him for death and a heavenly home.
Another kingdom rumbled in Judas's head
That would not come until this lord was dead.

John 6:70–71; John 13:26; Revelation 1:17–18

149

THE LORD OF THE SABBATH

Our Sabbath, resting like his Father God
After creation, he takes his ease and looks
Around, chewing the grain until it's gone.
Multitudes rush to him, for he can cook.
He speaks, and food appears in his human hand,
Meals that satisfy the hungry soul
Richer than manna white on desert sands.
Bread to die for; bread that will make us whole,
A banquet fit for a festive afternoon.
"Come unto me, and I will give you rest
Sweet as a summer nap in early June.
I'll be the host, and you will be my guest
Tippling in sunlight beside a crystal stream,
Waters that sparkle brighter than you can dream."

Matthew 12:1–8; Deuteronomy 23:25; 1 Samuel 21:1–6

150

THE MAN WITH A WITHERED HAND

Keeping the Sabbath for itself alone,
Misses out on the joy God means to give:
Odors of fresh bread wafting through the home,
The chores finished, all we need to live
Ready and waiting to fill us, make us glad.
Killjoys will frown at the candles and the feast,
Spurning our Father's gifts and getting mad.
The law is written to give us time to rest.
Jesus can see right through our pious airs.
He heals the withered hand to prove his point:
God prefers kindness to endless, showy prayers.
He works the miracle, and joint to joint,
The bones unravel, the fingers grow unclenched.
He breaks our rules to show us what Sabbath meant.

Matthew 12:9–13; Deuteronomy 22:4; 1 Kings 13:4

151

JESUS REBUKES THE RIGHTEOUS

An argument more modern than it seems,
The dietary laws are with us still.
Trusting that regimens of food will redeem
And save us; therefore all should do our will
And eat the menus we prescribe. He calls
Our legalisms out. It is the heart
That spews filth into the world. We brawl
Over figures drawn on colorful charts,
Buy indulgences with goods we ingest.
Meanwhile, corruptions from our mouths pollute
All of the natural things with which we're blest.
Keeping the rules but evil at the root,
Inciting hatred, vegetable rites
Rubbing the grain against our appetites.

Matthew 15:1–11; Ezekiel 33:31–33; 1 Corinthians 6:13

152

THE CANAANITE WOMAN
AND HER DAUGHTER

In a far country, out of Israel,
Jesus meets a woman who believes
He is "the Lord, the Son of David." She yells
For him to heal her daughter; she needs reprieve.
The demon never lets her rest; her cries
Irritate the disciples who beg the Lord
To send her away. He's silent. Then replies,
"I was not sent to you." She sinks to the floor,
"Help me!" A cry as plaintive as it gets.
"Even the dogs eat the table crumbs!"
Her faith surprises him. He sees a net
Singing across the waters, the kingdom come.
Her parable opens him to all the earth,
Stunned as she sees his wonder show its worth.

Matthew 15:21–28; Matthew 28:19–20; Romans 15:8

153

DEAF-MUTE AT DECAPOLIS

His friends brought a man who could not hear,
With a speech impediment, to Jesus. He touched
His ears, spit in his mouth, and sighed a prayer
To heaven. "Be opened!" It did not look like much,
But suddenly, the man could hear and speak
Clearly. The desert blossomed as a rose,
Isaiah's dreams fulfilled. He made the weak
Strong, the blind to see, the deaf man's woes
Vanish. "Tell no one!" said Jesus. Singing like a bird
All over town, the captive now is free.
He hears but does not listen to Christ's word
To keep quiet. The ancient prophecies
Are true. "Rejoice with me!" he moves his tongue,
"The finger of God wrote in my mouth a song."

Mark 7:31–37; Isaiah 35:1–8; Romans 4:16–18

154

ꜰEEDING THE ꜰOUR THOUSAND

He runs a mess hall next to a hospital,
Healing our bodies, then feeding us fresh food.
He knows our frame, like the grass of the fields,
Created in the garden, flesh and blood.
Three days listening, enraptured, they need lunch.
His heart goes out to them: before they faint
On their way home, they need a crust to munch.
"How much do you have?" The disciples, not yet saints,
Grumble, "Seven loaves and some fish."
Did they miss the miracle some days before
When Jesus served up a tasty dish?
Plenty for five thousand, many more,
The loaves and fish he handled multiplied,
Fish sandwiches for all the countryside.

Matthew 15:32–39; Acts 27:33–38; Romans 14:6–9

155

RELIGIOUS LEADERS DEMAND SIGNS

They want miracles from Jesus, signs
From heaven showing that he is truly God.
Jesus rebukes them, knowing that they are blind;
Though they can read the weather, what they cannot
Fathom is a miracle of his.
They would deny it, wondering what it meant.
Even the sign of Jonah, his spending three days
In the belly of the whale, the fundaments
Of hell, and then arising would not prove
Things they do not want the gift to see.
Only the eyes of faith are ever moved
By glimpses breaking from eternity.
Pure reason can never fathom that faith reveals
The grand veracities that facts conceal.

Matthew 16:1–4; Jonah 1:17; 1 Corinthians 1:22

156

RETURN ACROSS THE SEA

This is a failure to communicate—
Jesus is speaking of faith in metaphors
The disciples literally cannot relate.
"What is he talking about leaven for?
Have we run out of bread?" Jesus means
"Look out for bad doctrines of the holy crowd!
Like yeast, it will rise in your hearts unseen
And ruin the loaf; it cannot be sifted out.
The miracles of bread I made for you,
Were manna for your bodies and your souls,
A dinner cooked to fill you with my food,
To nourish all of you and make you whole.
Listen to the figures that I trace,
My leaven in your loaf, a saving grace."

Matthew 16:5–12; Romans 16:17–19; Galatians 5:9

157

BLIND MAN AT BETHSAIDA

Like the disciples in the boat, slow to learn,
This blind man's healing will take more time,
A couple tries. We see Jesus work
With those of little faith. These stories rhyme.
The man seems uncertain, somewhat weak in faith
When Jesus leads him away, out of town;
He holds him, spits into his eyes to bathe
The vacant pupils, wide irises of brown.
They open. He asks, "What do you see?"
"Men, but they look like trees walking," he says.
Christ puts his hand on his eyes tenderly.
His sight fully restored, Christ sends him away,
No word from him whose vision fills his eyes,
The tree of life beside him standing by.

Mark 8:22–26; Genesis 2:5–7; John 9:6

158

THE FEAST OF TABERNACLES

Remembering the time in the wilderness,
The harvest festival in Jerusalem.
Manna and water from the rock, a test
Of forty years wandering toward a dream,
The promised land, an emblem for our faith:
Waiting on God to give us everything,
Feeding and teaching us to meet our death.
A cloud of misty light, the staff, the spring,
Jesus is the bread, the water, and the light.
He will suffer the murmuring of the crowd.
All will oppose him, try to make him right;
He will hide himself inside a cloud.
A pillar of fire by night, a cloud by day,
The Light of the World appears to lead the way.

John 7:14–31; Exodus 40:34–38; Psalm 99:7

159

I AM THE WATER OF LIFE

Out of him gushes living water, springs,
Like rivers quenching the thirsty hearts of those
Who, parched, desire this fountain for their drink.
In the temple out of his body flow
Floods of the Spirit. The feast of booths,
Candles are glimmering over the temple wells
As Jesus cries out, I am the font of truth!
Few believe him; Where does this madman dwell?
Where does he come from? His brothers cannot say.
Legions of demons, mad, or one from God?
Never have they heard such talk. He is the way
Into the country he is speaking of—
A kingdom filling all with light forever,
The crystal stream beside the tree in heaven.

John 7:37–39; Leviticus 23:34–39; Isaiah 44:3–4

160

JESUS AND THE WOMAN
TAKEN IN ADULTERY

Their passions visible and ripe to stone,
She lay there weeping as their flesh took shape
Inside her womb, the body they had known,
Paid for, used up. Now they were ashamed.
She'd felt their lust, pushing and letting loose,
Their looming over her, her abject fear
Of issues burdening her; she could not choose
When they would leave behind a child to rear,
Born of a pressure she had come to dread.
Waiting there helpless, weeping at fate's decree,
The code she unlocked that ruled her feelings dead.
A voice stopped them. Lay down your arms, and read
The letters in the sand. Let mercy win.
They stood alone together without sin.

John 8:1–10; Leviticus 20:10; Ezekiel 16:38–40

161

BEFORE ABRAHAM, I AM

They thought the world would stop if he spoke the name:
"Before Abraham, I AM, the one God
Of your fathers, Isaac and Jacob, I am the same
As my Father." Blasphemy! How long
Can he go on? He looked like every man.
No prophet ever came from Nazareth;
Galilee was nothing. They could not understand
The shocking things this charlatan had said,
How he had mastered what they'd learned in school?
What were his credentials? He comprehended
More than their learned doctors, all their rules
Better than any. How could his work be ended?
Logic could not overcome his light
Gleaming from the holy city through the night.

John 8:39–59; Leviticus 24:15–15; Hebrews 11:13

162

I AM THE DOOR

"I AM the door," he said, "the way you enter
Into the perfect life." Open the gate,
Go straight ahead to the shining center
Of all creation, the object of your faith
Glowing like thousands of suns in a garden filled
With satisfying fruits, delights to taste.
Delectable, no labor in these fields.
All will be gathered by the gracious host
Who serves vintages as clear as glass
Colored with sunrise, burgundy and red,
Brimming with music sweeter than one could ask;
Miracles blossoming in their well-groomed beds.
You will be known; all will be recognized:
Walk through the lintels into paradise.

John 10:7–18; 1 Corinthians 13:8–13; Revelation 21:25

163

THE MAN BORN BLIND [A]

The dust of the earth made flesh when our Lord God
Knelt down and shaped in his image a living man;
Our Lord spat on the dust to form a clod
Of clay to replicate when life began
And rubbed mud on the eyes of the man born blind.
He went to wash them in Siloam's pool;
Dawn broke like the first day dancing in his mind.
He saw the Lord who'd read a deeper rule
So he could glorify his Father's name.
He caught us in our rigid pieties
Shocked by the fingers bursting into flame,
Burning away the darkness so he could see,
Opening our vision into all we know
Quickened, shining around us, bright as snow.

John 9:1–12; Exodus 20:5–6; Romans 13:12

164

THE MAN BORN BLIND [B]

"We must work," he said, "while it is day":
The light bursts into a blind man's sight,
And he sees. But his opponents say,
"We distrust him," and plummet into night.
Protesting the miracle, they all go dark,
Dead to what Christ the Light of the World has done.
How is it we cannot see or even mark
The brilliance of his work, the only Son?
Is there another world I cannot see
Until he anoints my eyes with his spit-filled mud?
Is that vision yet unborn in me?
Sometimes looking at the sparkling flood
Of sunlight that dazzles me and makes me blind,
A darkness as thick as midnight fills my mind.

John 9:13–41; 2 Thessalonians 1:11; Revelation 3:8

165

JESUS AT THE HOME OF
MARTHA AND MARY

Devout Mary sitting at Jesus' feet
Listens intently. Martha stands in the kitchen
Scowling. Mary gets points for being sweet—
While she is slaving away, they talk religion!
When she serves lunch, Martha upbraids the Lord.
"Mary should help me. I am all alone!"
What does he say? Does he have a word?
Can we understand his answer or hear his tone?
"She gets the better portion." He takes a piece,
A big bite out of Martha's harsh complaint
As he savors what she has baked. Is she pleased?
Martha is right; her sister is a saint.
Mary is feeding on Jesus' words for food;
Martha is cumbered about but understood.

Luke 10:38–42; Psalm 145:5; Revelation 22:8

166

CONfESSION Of pETEᴙ

Jesus asks the disciples, "Who do you say
I AM?" They look dumbfounded; who has got
The answer? Peter, of course, jumps into the fray:
"You are the Christ, the Son of the living God!"
"Blessed are you, Simon. My Father revealed
This truth to you. And I will build on this word
My church. The gates of hell will not prevail
Against it! The prophecies have been heard.
Now I must go up to Jerusalem
And suffer there. The elders, priests, and scribes
Will testify against me, all of them.
And there I will be scourged and crucified,
And on the third day, I will rise again.
Nothing will ever be what it has been!"

Matthew 16:13–28; Deuteronomy 5:26–27; 1 Corinthians 12:3

167

PETER, THE ROCK

Jesus chose Peter, the one on whom he'd build
His church. Petros, Cephas, like a rock.
Always ahead but often wrong, Christ willed
Imperfect Peter to lead his scraggly flock
To a new kingdom. Surely the Master knew
That Peter as first of all the living stones
Would be like all the other faithless crew,
Denials like facets on their craven bones.
He pointed to Peter, his confession enough
To shape cathedrals in his little lambs
Whom he rescued like diamonds in the rough.
We watch the walls rising, the great I AM
Constructing his church one broken rock at a time,
Healing each rift in the edges as he climbs.

Mark 8:27–38; 1 Corinthians 2:11–13; Hebrews 2:14–17

168

THE KEYS TO THE KINGDOM

Jesus gives Peter the keys to the kingdom of heaven,
A scene painters love; it's dramatic, the keys
Dangling between the two as Peter is given
A strange charge: How can a man bind and release
Another from sin? Is Peter standing there
At the pearly gates deciding yes or no?
It bothers us, having another declare
We are forgiven, electing where we'll go.
Absolution assures us God's word is true.
The door stands open. Have we by faith
Repented, stepped over the threshold, walked through,
Or are we standing outside in the courts of death,
Hearing the rusty key of the Law turn,
Locking in the wages we have earned?

Matthew 16:13–20; Isaiah 22:22–23; Revelation 1:17–18

169

GET BEHIND ME, SATAN

Peter is shocked when Jesus says he'll die
At the hands of the authorities. He reels
At the prophecy, his senses horrified:
The Son of God on a cross? Jesus heels
Back and rebukes him, "Get behind me, Satan!
Take my lead." Cephas was the rock,
Now he is worse than a faithless pagan
Who thinks he knows better. The Savior talks
Frankly: "I must do this for you," he says,
"I am the road that you must walk to find
The blessed path of true righteousness.
You cannot save me from this death. Get behind
Me, Peter. I go before you; do not stray.
I am the Lord. Follow in my way."

Matthew 16:21–23; Romans 8:5; Colossians 3:2

170

THE TRANSFIGURATION [A]

Brighter than eye can bear to see, he shines,
His face lighter than twenty suns, his clothes
Radiant with glory; they know he is divine.
Peter, James, and John watch as light glows
From his being, streaming with waves of light.
Moses and Elijah then appear;
They stand on the mountain talking, shining bright,
Their vocal frequencies too deep to hear,
The Law and Prophets next to the Son of God.
They disappear into a mist of sound.
Only a voice like the one that Moses heard
In the wilderness remains, casting them down.
"My beloved Son, in whom I'm well pleased,
Listen to him." Fathom divinity.

Matthew 17:1–8; Exodus 24:15–18; Daniel 7:9–10

171

THE TRANSFIGURATION [B]

Poor Peter! When he saw the three bathed in light,
He started talking: "Lord, it is good to be here!"
Wanting to do something, anything right,
Building three booths. He should be white with fear.
The glory of the Lord descends; a voice
Interrupts his chattering. The cloud
Thunders; they fall prostrate at the noise—
God speaks; creation trembles at the sound—
It dazzles them, like terror from the lost ark
Melting faces, tumbling them down in awe,
The grandeur of God's light more like the dark
Until Jesus touches them, saying, "Fear not!"
In the name of everything holy,
They look up and see Jesus only.

Mark 9:2–8; Deuteronomy 18:15; 2 Peter 1:15–21

172

A BOY POSSESSED BY A DEMON

"Listen to him!" Still ringing in their ears,
They go down the mountain and meet a man
With a son possessed by a demon. They hear
His story, how the boy thrashes about and lands
In fire or water, foaming at the mouth.
The disciples tried to heal him, but they failed.
Jesus grows angry, casts the demon out.
"Why did our prayers not work?" the disciples wail.
"Not enough faith," he says. "All you need
Is a tiny bit," then he rebukes them all:
"Even a faith tiny as a mustard seed
Can move mountains!" The seed is so small!
My little faith wants nothing less to prove
I can believe, a mountain Christ came to move.

Matthew 17:14–21; Zechariah 3:2; 1 Corinthians 12:9

173

JESUS PROPHESIES HIS DEATH A SECOND TIME

Ecstatic after his Transfiguration,
The disciples watch Jesus heal a boy.
Clearly their Master lords it over creation.
Astonishing, his power floods them with joy.
They had seen him on the mountain, dazzling light,
With Moses and Elijah, coming to believe
He is Messiah, but now after these heights,
Predicting a cruel death. They cannot perceive
What he is saying, the meaning hidden from them,
Their hearts hardened like Pharaoh's long ago.
Hearing Christ must die in Jerusalem,
They say nothing, frightened it might be so.
But how could this happen, this good man be killed?
They cannot believe it, so everyone keeps still.

Matthew 17:22–23; Exodus 11:10; Romans 5:8

174

COIN IN THE FISH'S MOUTH

Some fights are more important than other fights.
Going to the mat on the kind of music played
In church on Sunday, even if you're right,
Is useless; you build up a debt not easily paid.
Watch Peter pull out of a fish a coin
To save their fighting about the temple tax.
It got them off the hook, not having to join
Protests against minor stuff: relax!
Choose your battles, not everything is key.
Getting all hot and bothered over little things
Wearies people; you will never be free
Of causes. It's the words the singer sings
That matter. They should not take second place
And cause the worshipper a fit of grace.

Matthew 17:24–27; Amos 5:21–24; Romans 13:7

175

THE UNFORGIVING SERVANT

Like the unjust steward, we owe our Lord
More than all the treasure in the world.
Empires of gold and silver cannot afford
The price of our redemption—rubies, pearls—
Nothing can pay the debt we have to face.
Weeping to be set free from all we owe,
We say, release me, and look to him for grace.
He graciously redeems us. Paid up, we go
To the one we lent a little sum to help
Buy groceries when she had no ready cash.
Spendthrifts we need her money; we see ourselves
As poor, not rich in mercy; we use the lash.
Unregenerate from the very start,
With not a stitch of credit in our hearts.

Matthew 18:23–35; Leviticus 25:39–44; Proverbs 21:13

176

JESUS PREVENTED FROM TRAVELING THROUGH SAMARIA

Like Isaiah, Christ set his face like flint
Toward Jerusalem, the time growing near
For him to be taken up. Some tried to prevent
His passage through Samaria; they were clear
He'd spark trouble, disrupting the status quo.
The Sons of Thunder wanted to call fire down
To consume them, like Elijah long ago.
Jesus rebuked them, staying in another town.
They kindle phrases against them, burning with rage,
Red embers crackling, hard to understand,
But old wounds never heal from age to age;
From the prophets to Jesus, revealing more of his plans,
The portents clearer with each step they take,
The truth taking fire, showing much is at stake.

Luke 9:51–56; 2 Kings 1:9–12; Isaiah 50:7

177

CLEANSING THE TEN LEPERS [A]

They knew him, from far off, calling him by name,
"Jesus, Master," their voices hoarse from disease.
He saw them, all ten, quarantined by shame.
Without touching them, he sent them to the priest
To be declared clean. They knew the rules,
The measures from Leviticus, the rite
To bring them home. Quickly their ardor cooled.
Going for their exam, what was it like?
Noses growing back, their toes restored,
Rotten flesh healed, no need to shout unclean,
Their keenest nerves knitting together, the Lord
Left behind as they fingered their new skin,
Walking back to health, into a new day,
Each hurt more distant every step of the way.

Luke 17:11–14; Leviticus 13:2–3; 2 Kings 5:1–14

178

CLEANSING THE TEN LEPERS [B]

Rejoicing as they felt that they were cleansed,
They went their separate ways, all but one.
A foreigner came back, leaving his friends;
Gratitude shone from him like the noonday sun.
Praises to God flowed from his grateful heart.
He fell on his face before Jesus, giving thanks;
Joy burbling in his body, sound in every part.
Jesus wondered at the missing ranks
Of the nine others, giddy with joy and whole.
His own missing the miracle again;
He peered deeply into the grateful soul
And saw a double blessing in the man:
His body healed, his faith had made him well
And saved him, stories the man would live to tell.

Luke 17:15–19; Numbers 16:22; Psalm 103:1–3

179

SEVENTY DISCIPLES

Two by two he sent them to every town:
"Announce the kingdom of God is near to you,
Take nothing along, say in every house,
'The peace of God be here.' See what they do.
If they receive you, eat and drink with them;
If not, shake the dust off your weary feet
And leave." They returned praising his name;
Joyfully, they recited all their deeds.
Jesus saw Satan tumbling from paradise,
The seventy with Moses, the sapphire floor
Shimmering in the bright cerulean skies,
All of us feasting together, an open door,
Glimpses of God's eternity come clear,
Bringing the rim of heaven's portals near.

Luke 10:1–20; Exodus 24:9–11; Revelation 21:10–14

180

THE FATHER WORKS IN SECRET

The Father works in secret, and he hides
Truths from the learned but to the least makes known
All of the wisdom anyone needs to guide
The way to the Father. The wise cannot be shown
The simple things; they want it to be hard,
Complicated, so only they understand.
They hoard their knowledge, keeping it under guard
Like Knights Templar traipsing through every land
Looking for the Holy Grail, missing the cup
The pastor holds out to them in church.
They like to make obscure theories up.
Hoping to crack a code, they search and search,
Spurning the simple means of grace that save,
The open secret in an empty grave.

Luke 10:21–24; 1 Corinthians 1:26–31; Hebrews 11:13

181

PARABLE OF THE GOOD SAMARITAN

He fell among thieves who left him there for dead,
Stripped of his money, clothes, or breath itself
Alone. He lay bleeding, stones for a bed—
Easy to pass him by and not to help—
The clergy on their way to doing good
Had rules to follow. All the cleansing rites
Take time. A passing outcast understood,
Moved by compassion, afraid the man would die.
A good neighbor, one who shows mercy on
The suffering, something I should want to do,
But here I lie helpless in the hot sun
Unable to lift a finger. Lord, I cry for you,
An outcast, my neighbor, to bandage up my sores
Filling my heart with mercies from your store.

Luke 10:30–37; Leviticus 22:1–7; James 2:14–17

182

DIVORCE AND CELIBACY

The attorney in us will argue here:
Moses changed the law concerning divorce,
Establishing a loophole, making clear
It could be legal, necessary of course.
But Jesus set creation over man's law,
Since generation is the key to life.
The legal codes are made to hedge our flaws.
When God created husbands to seek a wife,
He planned their congress so life would carry on
And blesses marriage so we grow and flourish,
Passing down through our daughters and our sons
Habits written into flesh that nourish
Children and raise them; it's how we've tried to live
From the moment Adam first saw Eve.

Matthew 19:1–9; Genesis 1:31; Genesis 2:21–24

183

THE LITTLE CHILDREN

"Who is the greatest in the kingdom of heaven?"
The disciples wonder. Jesus grabs a child
From the crowd, holds it, and then he gives them
A lesson. The child is greatest, weak or wild,
Not because it's innocent, but small,
Needing to be tended, disciplined,
Looking to her parents for comfort when she calls
For someone to say the monsters are only wind,
Who waits upon his father's hands for food,
Her mother teaching her how to behave,
To look to heaven for everything that's good.
Trusting our Father for everything we have,
Like children reaching for dad to pick them up,
Bathed in the pleasures of their mother's love.

Matthew 19:13–15; Psalm 131:2; 3 John 1:4

184

JESUS AND THE RICH YOUNG MAN

The rich young man could buy anything,
Have whatever his youthful heart desired.
He wanted eternal life, like a gold ring,
A commodity to be sold to the richest buyer.
Jesus changes the terms. It is a way
Of life, a house you enter, a place to live,
Following the commandments every day.
It cannot be bought; it is something Jesus gives,
Something only those who lose can find.
When he has sold his stuff, given to the poor,
Then he will get it, the changing of his mind.
His clutter gone, he can open the door
To a treasure trove in heaven, where he will get
Forgiveness of all his unacknowledged debt.

Matthew 19:16–22; Leviticus 18:1–5; Nehemiah 9:29–30

185

THE EYE OF THE NEEDLE

"It is easier for a camel to pass through
The eye of a needle than for a person who is rich
To enter the kingdom of heaven." Then who
Can be saved? the disciples asked, raising their pitch.
He speaks the truth. Riches and the kingdom of heaven
Point two different ways. They do not lead
One to another. We know the wealth we're given
Can become our god, gold an aching need
That takes devotion away from our Lord.
Riches cumber us with lots of stuff.
Our spending reveals the things our hearts adore,
All of it dross, none of it enough
To save us. Jesus' hyperbole is clear:
Only God's mercy brings the kingdom near.

Matthew 19:23–30; James 5:1–6; Revelation 3:17–19

186

THE WORKERS IN THE VINEYARD

One goes 'round and around on this strange tale:
The master is honest; he paid what he agreed
To the longest-working laborers; they rail,
Realizing their time sweating in the weeds
Earned them the same wages as those who worked
Barely an hour. It did not seem fair.
The master argued he had kept his word:
"Friends, am I not free to pay the same share
To each? Do not begrudge the way I think."
Seen from the point of view of heaven's grace—
Which never reckons the labor in its drink—
How can a cup hold more than it has space?
All portions are the same and quite enough
To quit our haggling over measures of love.

Matthew 20:1–16; Leviticus 19:13; Romans 6:20–23

187

I AM THE GOOD SHEPHERD

Scenes of Jesus as the Shepherd are sweet;
The tiny lamb in his arms is cute.
Though all we know of lamb today is meat,
Sheep are not among the most astute.
What they do is hear their shepherd's voice
And follow him. If they wander off,
Away from him, the shepherd has no choice
But to search for them up through crags and bluffs
To find them before predators, like wolves,
Sharp-toothed and hungry, slay them and eat them up.
He lays down his life to find us silly fools,
Bleating in the darkness, hoping against hope;
He'll reach into our terror and take us back
To the green pastures where we will nothing lack.

John 10:7–18; Luke 15:1–10; Psalm 23

188

JESUS REBUKES THE
PHARISEES AND SCRIBES

"Hypocrisy is the homage vice pays
To virtue," La Rochefoucauld once said. Why clean
Only the outside of a cup? It says
We try to keep our vice from being seen.
When someone comes to drink from it and finds
It's filthy, it will tell them who we are.
We know their moral compass, how their minds
Work, enough to play charades. How far
Must we dissemble to show that we are good?
We know being a hypocrite is wrong.
But still we masquerade, do what we should
So they think we are something else all along.
We pull a fast one to keep them from finding out
That truly we are false; there's little doubt.

Luke 11:37–41; 2 Corinthians 11:13–15; Titus 1:15–16

189

ETERNAL SIN

Loving our sin more than we love God,
Making an idol of it, shutting down
The cry of conscience, holding nothing in awe,
Crowning ourselves with the solemnest of crowns—
The sin against the Holy Spirit begins
Wherever hearts are hardened against the voice
Whispering to them, Repent, repent, this sin.
We silence it and make a dreadful choice,
No grief, no sorrow over the pain we cause,
No wondering whether we should have stopped to think
When hurting another, we flout and break the laws,
Not caring about pushing one over the brink—
Our own monarchs, we will rule the day;
Not even our court jester has much to say.

Matthew 12:30–32; Hebrews 6:4–6; 1 John 5:16–17

190

THE RICH FOOL

A farmer once rejoiced to see his fields
Produce more grain than he could ever store.
He built more barns to hold these fruitful yields.
With granaries packed full, no longer poor,
He took his ease, sat back, addressed himself,
"Soul, you'll never need to work again;
Eat, drink, be merry, trust in your own wealth,
Depending on the labors of other men . . ."
Out of the whirlwind, a voice thundered, "Look out!
The riches you have stored cannot sustain
Life beyond the veil where no one counts
Bushels or silos heaped with golden grain.
Only a fool would think he could invest
Things of this world for interest in the next."

Luke 12:16–21; 1 Samuel 25:1–42; Ecclesiastes 9:7–12

191

THE fAITHfUL SERVANT

Keep your lamps trimmed and burning, Jesus says,
Always ready for his return like a thief
In the night. It will be a great surprise:
To many horror; to others a relief.
Do nothing special; don't sell your goods to wait
On a hilltop, a time you cannot know; prepare
By always being ready. Knowing the date
Could make you slothful, beware, beware.
Not even the Son nor the angels know
The day nor the hour. Keep planting crops
That take years to mature, their fruitage slow.
Only the Father knows when time will stop.
The Lord would find you faithful most of all,
Your lamps burning brightly in the wedding hall.

Luke 12:35–40; Daniel 2:21; 1 Thessalonians 5:2–11

192

THE WICKED SERVANTS

Faithful servants do their duty and feed
The household in due season; they bring God's word
To the hungry, they know the wants and needs
Of those they care for, they believe the Lord
Will soon return—they would be ready for him.
Knowing he is close at hand restrains
His servants from acting on every sinful whim.
But thinking he tarries, they start raising Cain,
Killing their futures, losing their faith to drink,
Reveling in the gods of here and now;
No longer fearful, they stand upon the brink
Of judgment. New prophets see this, fearing how
Failing to believe that Christ is coming soon
Brings dissolution, violence, and doom.

Luke 12:41–48; Numbers 15:30; 1 Corinthians 15:30–34

193

THE TOWERS OF SILOAM

Cruel tyrants, like Herod, can kill the innocent,
Practice abominations, and terrify
Their citizens with random punishments.
Nature can be wanton; its gorgeous vistas lie
Spread out for us to wonder at and then
Houses flying in the winds over the land.
Has God's wrath ripped them up to punish sin?
Jesus resists this way to understand
Catastrophes that end in pain and death,
But be ready, repent, amend your ways.
When the waters wash over you and take your breath
And suddenly you face the end of your days,
Yours not to find the cause, but be prepared
For the last moment when you haven't got a prayer.

Luke 13:1–4; Zephaniah 1:14–18; Galatians 6:7–10

194

THE BARREN FIG TREE

The farmer says, "This tree is barren; cut
It down. Some think it's pretty in the spring,
But even with fresh blossoms, if there's no fruit,
Chop it down; let the axes ring.
I need the ground for useful crops to grow,
To bring to market produce I can sell.
A farmer does not plant a tree for show.
My neighbor loves it; its fragrant April smell—
'Keep it,' he says, 'I'll tend it like my son,
Nurture and train it up so it will bear
Harvests of plenty when the autumn comes.
Give me some time; wait another year.'
If he wants to save it, I will let him try,
But turn it into kindling if it dies."

Luke 13:6–9; Ezekiel 18:30; 2 Peter 1:8

195

AN INFIRM WOMAN

We see her bent over double and want to say,
"Be free, stand up straight, you have been healed."
Would all hell break loose if one day
It happened here? Would it be taken for real?
A miracle confounds logic. We jump
To explain it, but the scandal remains:
A chaplain, under fire, dove into a dump,
Broke his back. "You'll never walk again,"
The doctor, a full bird colonel, said. He knelt
Beside him. "Are you a praying man?" he asked.
"God, heal him." The reverend walked but did not tell
A soul. He never talked about his past.
As he lay dying, he told his student nurse,
Who preaches every chapter, every verse.

Luke 13:10–17; Psalm 116:16–17; Ezekiel 46:1–4

196

THE FIRST SHALL BE LAST

The guests at heaven's banquet may be a surprise:
Abraham, Isaac, and Jacob will be there,
All of the prophets, but will we recognize
Complete strangers? Will we be prepared
To welcome those from north, south, west, and east,
Many we may have judged without respect,
Those out of favor, outcasts, the very least?
The worthies knocking at the gate expect
Some recognition. Alas, they are not known.
There is no rank or order at the end;
Only those whom Christ has called his own,
Who gladly follow him and are his friends,
May enter. The hierarchies of worth are past:
By faith, the last may be first, the first be last.

Luke 13:22–30; Psalm 6:8–9; Matthew 25:12–13

197

JERUSALEM, JERUSALEM

On his way up to Jerusalem
From Galilee, Jesus hears Herod seeks
To kill him. Jesus makes it clear to them
He fears nothing. "Tell that fox I'll speak
And heal, driving out demons as I go,"
Taunting the tyrant, knowing he will die
In the holy city where he will meet the foe
And do battle. In agony, he cries,
"Jerusalem! Jerusalem! You kill
The prophets; your children suffer for no good.
O that I could hold them close and still,
Like a mother hen gathers up her brood
Under her wings to keep them safe and sound,
But you would not let me." Watch, the fox coming 'round.

Luke 13:31–35; Deuteronomy 32:11–12; Lamentations 2:13

198

MAN WITH DROPSY

Swollen with edema, he stood right there
Looking at them, crashing the Sabbath meal.
He saw them feasting with Jesus. He needed care;
Everyone knew he was asking to be healed.
Conversation stopped as they watched;
What would he do? Would he break the rule?
They'd argued this before, their reasons botched.
So they kept silent. Jesus was no fool.
He named their quibbles, making the argument,
"Would you not care for your oxen or your son
If they fell into a well?" They saw what he meant
As he went to heal the man. Everyone
Looked down, hearing floods of water rush
Out of his body; their vexed faces flushed.

Luke 14:1–6; Deuteronomy 22:4; Psalm 103:1–5

199

COUNTING THE COST

It's costly, following this Lord. He wants
All of you. Doing his will may separate
Parents from children, husbands from wives, old aunts
From dear nieces and nephews. It may feel like hate
To those left behind. Missionaries knew
These verses well as they waved their last goodbyes
To parents fluttering hankies, dropping from view
To the creaking axles, salt blurring their eyes.
Like Stan Quanbeck, still a small boy, alone
When his sister died, after his parents left
For the Malagasy bush, without a phone.
Only orchids he came to loathe, bereft
Of his mother's arms. And still he served his Christ,
Whose riches somehow paid this awful price.

Luke 14:25–27; Deuteronomy 33:8–9; Acts 20:24–27

200

THE LOST SHEEP

A shepherd tending sheep, the little ones
Safe in his arms, the still waters beside
Green pastures: sheep grazing, ambling in the sun,
Scampering onward, bleating for a guide.
The complications of this image shift.
He gives his life to find the lost, the stray.
Spending himself, scaling the rocky rifts
To rescue us from falling, falling away
Just before we tumble into death.
It spins again; he turns into the lamb
Leading us like a staff of hope and faith.
He goes before us, the sacrificial ram.
We see him take our place over the abyss,
Relieved as Isaac watching the embers hiss.

Luke 15:1–7; Zechariah 13:7; Psalm 23

201

THE LOST COIN

When he looked up into the starry heavens,
He saw the angels rollicking over one
Repentant sinner who had been forgiven,
Novas exploding with joy. He'd begun
Dreaming of China, whose hundred millions called
For him to bring them Jesus, each twinkling star
A seraph dancing through the crystal halls
Of paradise for one who'd come from afar
Into the courts of light. He wanted to add
Thousands, burning lanterns for each new soul.
Rocking back on his heels, his heart was glad,
Rejoicing under the sparkling starlit dome,
Looking east into the end of night
Pearling with dawn, more stars hidden by light.

Luke 15:8–10; Acts 1:6–8; Acts 26:13–23

202

PARABLE OF THE PRODIGAL

Even if we had not heard this story,
We know it well. Most of us wanted our way,
Wishing to flee our home territory,
Family, friends, neighbors and not obey
Our parents' wishes. We wanted to be on our own,
Take our inheritance, leaving our folks in tears.
Kind, they help us pack, give us a car and phone.
Our reassurances do not calm their fears
As we roar off into an unknown world.
Their persistent prayers for us rise up:
"Lord, help them flourish, find friends, boys and girls
Good for them." They weep, hoping against hope
We will not waste our living on gaudy things
Nor suffer the consequence such rashness brings.

Luke 15:11–32; Deuteronomy 21:15–17; Proverbs 2:1–5

203

THE PRODIGAL

Springtime. The world fresh and green, he drove
Away, top down, a full bank account
Of his own, a ready monetary trove.
He got the best apartment to be found,
Stocked the finest vintages he could buy,
Read up on all the right places to go.
Rich as Solomon but not as wise,
He tasted much of life, both high and low,
Treating his companions to lavish gifts,
Wasting his substance on things that could not last.
Strange to delaying satisfaction or thrift,
His fortune ran through his fingers lightning fast.
Suddenly, he could not pay his monthly rent,
His heritage and living wasted, spent.

Luke 15:11–32; Proverbs 5:7–14; 1 Peter 4:1–4

204

THE PRODIGAL SON

Thrown out of his digs, hooked on lethal drugs,
He landed on the street, begging for food,
Vulnerable to dangerous, violent thugs,
In and out of jail, bad neighborhoods.
He found a job tending hogs on a farm,
Feeding them and shoveling manure.
Miserable and hungry, he wanted something warm,
His mother's home cooking, soup du jour.
Throwing dry cobs of corn to the pigs,
He came to himself: "Even my father's help
Eats better than I. I will go home and beg
To be a servant in his house myself."
He rose up from the sty and began to move
Past the forsaken premises of his loves.

Luke 15:13–19; 2 Chronicles 33:11–13; Revelation 7:16–17

205

THE PRODIGAL DECIDES TO GO HOME

He rehearsed the speech, regretting all he had done:
"Father, I have sinned against heaven and you.
I am no longer worthy to be called your son."
Every prophecy they made had come true.
Hunger drove him onward, but shame blushed
Over him, wondering if they'd let him stay.
Once again, the words in his heart rushed
Out of him: "I am not worthy." What would they say?
The golden fields beside him stretched on for miles,
Combines winnowing clouds of yellow chaff
Into the blue sky. The bus stopped. In a little while,
The door opened with a lurch, and he stepped off
Into the afternoon, ripples of heat
Rising from his brother's share, the ripe wheat.

Luke 15:15–20; Exodus 10:16; 1 Kings 8:46–51

206

THE PRODIGAL COMES HOME

He saw the bus stop out on the county road,
A figure holding a bag. Through long years,
He'd watched for this. The way the person strode,
He knew him. He was alive despite their fears.
He rose up from the lawn chair, running as fast
As his old bones could move down the dusty lane.
Not a thought about the wait, the past.
It was life to see his child again.
The knees on his jeans worn through, his shirt
Buttons missing, too big, lost in its shroud,
He approached, looking down at the dirt,
Ashamed. Clearing his throat to speak aloud,
"Father," he mumbled but could not say a thing;
His father kissed him, burbling of robes and rings.

Luke 15:20–24; 2 Samuel 14:33; 2 Corinthians 7:10–11

207

THE PARTY FOR THE PRODIGAL

The father called them all to celebrate,
To kill the fattened calf and have a feast.
"Invite the neighbors in, open the gate,
Welcome them all, the highest to the least.
Get a band to play, singers to sing;
Let's have a party! I thought my son was dead!
He has been raised! Give him the signet ring,
New suit, a cap upon his wounded head.
We did not think he would ever return.
He's here, not rotting in an unmarked tomb.
Dance with me like the stars when he was born.
Turn up the volume! Fill up his empty room.
Help him forget the horrors he has seen.
He's been to hell and back; let the revels begin."

Luke 15:22–24; Genesis 41:42; Esther 3:10

208

THE PRODIGAL'S OLDER BROTHER

Out in the fields harvesting the grain,
He heard the revels sounding, raucous cries.
Strange, his father had not entertained
For years, mourning as if someone had died.
The hired man told him, "Your brother has come home
Safely; your father killed the fattened calf
To celebrate." He spat, "I will not come
To the party. I worked hard to deserve the half
That belongs to me." His father came to entreat
His dutiful son to join them. "You never gave
Even a goat for me to enjoy a feast
With my friends. Now this bum, this knave,
Returns after wasting your holdings on prostitutes.
And still you squander mercy on his suits?"

Luke 15:25–30; Proverbs 29:3; 2 Timothy 1:4–7

209

THE PRODIGAL FATHER

The father, standing by his older son,
Out in the late afternoon light,
"You are always with me; my will is done:
All that is mine is yours. It is right
To celebrate. Your brother has come back!
Rejoice; we believed that he was dead,
But he's alive; the lost is found. Give thanks.
Come home; together, let us break some bread."
How he answered him we are not told.
Would we be sorry to see the joy in his face,
Go back to our work, reaping the fields of gold,
Jealous for the folly of our father's grace,
Or follow behind the old man's plodding steps
Over the stubble to the company he kept?

Luke 15:31–32; John 8:35; Romans 8:12–17

210

THE UNJUST STEWARD

Shocking to hear, this parable of Christ—
He recommends to us a dishonest man
Making provision for his future. Wise
In finance, he has the smarts to write a plan
Ensuring he will have enough to live
When he is old, cheating to be secure.
So also as children of light, we should give
Thought to our endings. What we spend makes clear
Where our heart is. Mammon can lead us astray
Toward nothing. If we follow in the light,
Heaven appears. We cannot travel two ways.
Be shrewd in both worlds. If we do right
And show our prudence, investing our treasures well,
In everlasting mansions where we will dwell.

Luke 16:1–13; 1 Corinthians 9:17; 1 Timothy 6:9–10

211

THE RICH MAN AND LAZARUS [A]

The rich man dressed in purples feasted inside
His house; outside his gate lay Lazarus
Begging for crumbs the rich man did not provide.
Covered with sores—wild dogs licked the pus—
He died; angels carried Lazarus up
To Abraham's bosom. The rich man died and went
To Hades, tormented by flames, without hope.
He cried out to Abraham, "Father, send
Lazarus with a drop of water to cool
My tongue." The way was closed, the tables turned.
He had ignored the poor man, the rich old fool.
No relief for him as the hellfires burn;
He faces the consequence of his neglect,
Eternity to reckon its effects.

Luke 16:19–31; Esther 8:15; James 5:1–5

212

THE RICH MAN AND LAZARUS [B]

The rich man lived sumptuously and ignored
Lazarus, ending up in flames.
The moral of this story of our Lord
Is clear. Missing the truth of the poor man's claim
Doomed him to eternal suffering.
Jesus uses it to help us see
Those on the corner begging, to whom we fling
Dollars to ease our conscience and their pleas.
Albert Schweitzer said this parable
Called him to Africa. A man of parts,
He left his tenure. It was unbearable
For him to live in riches and miss the heart
Of this lesson. In it, the scholar heard
A call to live in concert with Christ's word.

Luke 16:19–31; Acts 3:2; Revelation 18:16

213

THE RICH MAN AND LAZARUS [C]

"Send Lazarus to my brothers so they repent,"
Said the rich man to Abraham, "All five!"
Hell's chasm could not be crossed; one must be sent
Back from the bosom of Abraham alive.
Will they believe a risen man's report,
Having read in Moses and the prophets
Their obligations to the sick and poor?
That is enough. But if none of them saw fit
To follow Moses and treat their neighbors right,
Why listen to a man raised from the dead?
Preachers ask this question as they write
Sermons to give witness to what Scripture says,
That Jesus Christ is risen and standing here:
Will anyone wake up and see him near?

Luke 16:19–31; Psalm 17:14; 2 Timothy 4:1–5

214

HURTING LITTLE CHILDREN

Better a millstone be hung around your neck
And you be drowned in the sea than hurt a child.
Jesus has no pity on those who molest
An innocent so they feel hurt, defiled.
Causing the little child to lose its faith.
Such deserve the lowest place in hell.
It's worse than killing someone; a thousand deaths
Follow when you make a little one dwell
In terror, fighting memories of hurt,
Ending up rejecting the love of Christ
Because you harmed them in secret, unobserved,
Exacting on their person a terrible price.
They pay over and over for hurt you caused
When, without mercy, you broke the Savior's laws.

Matthew 18:1–6; 1 Corinthians 8:12; 2 Timothy 3:1–5

215

THE MASTER AND THE SERVANT

Servants do their duty; it is their call
To do what is expected; we should not earn
Trophies for being faithful, that is all
Our Lord expects, a lesson for us to learn.
Wanting praise for doing what we should,
Thinking we are owed a thank you card
For faithful service, for doing something good
Is folly; God does not pass out rewards
But lavishes grace on us because of love,
Not to pay us back for our good deeds.
To think that we could ever do enough
To earn a crumb of mercy that we need
For our sins and shortcomings is to miss
What beggars we are; how great God's mercy is.

Luke 17:7–10; 1 Samuel 12:24; Ecclesiastes 12:13–14

216

THE KINGDOM OF GOD
IS IN YOUR MIDST

Wherever Jesus is, the kingdom's there.
They cannot see it and need to have a sign.
Thinking he has a strategy prepared,
His satraps can follow line by dismal line.
But it is unseen, the kingdom that he builds,
For he has joined the heavens to the earth
In his own human flesh; the Godhead fills
His being to bring eternal things to birth.
When he speaks, deep in our cells, we hear the sound
Our corpuscles know of one who drew
The alphabets together and wrote them down.
He makes us consonant with all things new
And brings eternity into our hearts,
Realities our gadgets cannot chart.

Luke 17:20–21; Romans 14:17–19; Revelation 5:9–10

217

THE CONSUMMATION OF THE KINGDOM

Jesus says he will return like a great big flash
Of lightning. Everyone will see it at once
And run for cover, screaming as they dash
Back to their houses, swept away, as they run,
By the floods, swallowed up as things go dark,
Dying for life. So be ready, prepare, prepare!
When Noah's family finally boarded the ark,
Everyone scoffed and went to do their hair,
Feed the oxen, going about their lives.
The rain flooded the earth, and all were drowned.
All except Noah, his three sons, and their wives.
Vultures will gather where the corpse is found.
Save your lives now; repent and enter in
To a new life made for you. Let it begin.

Luke 17:22–37; Amos 5:18–19; 1 Thessalonians 4:13–18

218

THE UNJUST JUDGE

A white night in Luebeck, after church,
Heels clicking on the cobblestones.
We'd been singing hymns of Christ's return.
Old bells chiming quarters in dulcet tones.
"Why does he tarry? It's been so long," she asked.
The man in the moon sailing above us winked,
Laughter drifted across the square, a flask
Of wine lay in the gutter, we'd heard it clink
To fragments, its bouquet hanging in the air.
"The unrighteous judge finally did relent
And gave in to the anxious widow's prayer."
Two thousand years is time enough, she meant.
Off in the distance, a frantic siren wailed.
A warning, an ending, be faithful, do not fail.

Luke 18:1–8; Genesis 6:5–7; 1 Corinthians 1:4–9

219

THE RIGHTEOUS AND THE SINNER

Few of us brag about the good we do
To show ourselves better than anyone else
Even if quietly we think it's true.
Numbering like prayer beads the times we've helped
The poor, worked a food line, found a place
For an addict, read Bible stories to a child,
Proud to be deserving of God's grace.
These lists of credits, deeds of love required
By the master, are not the ticket in
To glory. Only repentance, crying to God,
"Have mercy on me a sinner, for I have sinned,"
Brings us into the presence of heaven's love
That sends us out to the world to do some good,
Praying to help despite our rectitude.

Luke 18:9–14; Ezra 9:6; Revelation 3:17

The Raising of Lazarus

220

THE RAISING OF LAZARUS [A]

A sick man, Lazarus, whom Jesus loved,
Brother to Mary and Martha in Bethany,
Was dying. The sisters knew it was enough
To send one sentence to Jesus and simply say,
"The one you love is ill." Believers, their prayer
A model. They told their master what was true,
Only the bare facts. They knew he cared
For them, so refrained from telling him what to do.
He had driven the demons out and healed
Every kind of ailment; miracles of bread
Dropped from his hands into baskets to make a meal
For thousands, but could he raise one from the dead?
They trusted him, their faith beyond a doubt,
Praying to save their brother from his shroud.

John 11:1–3; Matthew 10:38–39; Jude 1:20–22

221

THE RAISING OF LAZARUS [B]

The messenger arrived, sweaty with news
Of Lazarus; Jesus figured he was dead,
But prophesied the sisters would not lose.
"This illness will not lead to death," he said,
"But glorify the Father and his Son."
Cryptic on the facing of a tomb,
Outrageous. His disciples, every one,
Knew but one dimension. The man was doomed
To rot inside his grave, fed by stones,
Lying beside his father's fetid corpse,
A redolent reunion of family bones
Dressed in the putrid linens they last wore.
But Jesus saw a glory in this tale,
One that would shine forever beyond the pale.

John 11:4; Psalm 30:3; 1 Corinthians 15:17–21

222

THE RAISING OF LAZARUS [C]

Jesus does not come; he delays
Going to Bethany to see his friends,
Waiting before leaving two full days.
What are his purposes, his holy ends?
His watch is set to a different zone.
He will arrive at exactly the right hour.
While we are crying, it seems, to ears of stone,
Our Lord is making ready. The bell in the tower
Chimes; he appears, bushels of miracles
In his nail-pierced hands. To heal the sick,
Raise the dead, empty the rocky hulls
Honeycombing the town, send old Nick
Back to the teeming colonies of hell,
Where out of time, his busy minions dwell.

John 11:5–6; Isaiah 44:24–26; 2 Peter 3:8–10

223

THE RAISING OF LAZARUS [D]

Jesus' talk of night and day, of sleep
And death, mystifies the twelve. They ask
What on earth he means; climbing the steeps
Of language—is he using it to mask
The truth, calling death sleep to calm their fear?
To go to Bethany is to face their doom.
But death cannot do its work when he is near.
Jesus is the last word in any room;
He is the Son come from heav'n, the world's true light,
The mortal enemy of sin and death.
The torches and lanterns they will brandish in the night
Pale in his presence; he spans the lengths and breadths
Of many worlds and knows what words are for,
For Jesus sleep is not a metaphor.

John 11:9–13; Jeremiah 13:16; Hosea 6:1–3

224

THE RAISING OF LAZARUS [E]

When Thomas hears what Jesus means by sleep,
He says, "Then let us go and die with him."
Has all their talk forced him to scan the deeps
Of being killed in Jerusalem?
Thomas, the doubter, the man of little faith,
Believes now that Jesus is going to die.
In Bethany, Christ will fix his fate,
Unwrapping the deepest powers and where they lie.
"Ungodly!" We cry against our God and worse.
Threatening the temples we build, Christ is
The Lord that structures all the universe,
Death falls before him, all creation his.
Does Thomas see in the stir his Master caused
The one who formed them from dust and wrote their laws?

John 11:12–16; Genesis 2:7; 2 Corinthians 6:16–18

225

THE RAISING OF LAZARUS [f]

Martha active, Mary contemplative,
Used for centuries to describe
Various ways for Christian saints to live
And be faithful. Here we see Martha's drive,
Running to meet Jesus the first she hears
He has come. Naturally, she reprimands
The Savior. "If you had only been here,
My brother would not have died!" She demands
An answer. Still she trusts him and believes
Jesus could have healed Lazarus,
But raise him? Her voice rises and falls with grief.
We love her for the way she starts to fuss.
Her faith crying out to the Lord in pain,
Confident he won't mind her raising Cain.

John 11:20–27; Colossians 3:4; 1 Peter 1:20–21

226

THE RAISING OF LAZARUS [G]

Martha knows the half of it. "God will give
Whatever you ask." "He will rise again,"
Says Jesus. She thinks on the last day he will live,
But he is saying more than other men.
"I AM the resurrection and the life."
She knows the divine name and hears his claim
That those who trust in him will never die.
Seeing it whole, nothing will be the same.
"You are the Christ, the Son of God, the one
Who is coming into the world." As she confessed
Jesus the Messiah who is God's Son,
She shook up everything. Her name be blest.
Busy Martha vexed by Mary's sloth
Sweeps away disbelief with a dusty cloth.

John 11:27; 1 Corinthians 15:42–49; Philippians 3:20–21

227

THE RAISING OF LAZARUS [H]

Back home weeping, Mary hears the Lord
Is calling for her. She rises up and runs,
Falling before the Savior's feet. Her words,
The same as her sister's, what he might have done
If he had been prompter. She and her friends wept
Loudly. Mary is too sensitive;
She takes it personally. Why had he kept
Away? Lazarus would be alive
If he'd not tarried. Mourning on the path,
Their keening like sharp blades piercing the air,
Her tears burden him, seeing death's aftermath.
Listening to the groaning of their anguished prayers,
He gazes into Mary's crestfallen face,
Where all her contemplations can be traced.

John 11:28–33; Psalm 6:1–10; Psalm 30:5

228

THE RAISING OF LAZARUS [1]

Seeing Mary and her friends in tears
Moves Jesus deeply, and he begins to weep,
Thinking of the tomb, the sum of all our fears.
Earlier he had taught this death was sleep
And moments later would call out to the corpse
"Come forth!" But now with the mourners he wept,
Sobbing with grief like he'd never done before.
Into all human agony he'd stepped,
Born to battle sin, death, and the devil,
To break through the impediments of a stone.
All of the sorrows of mortal flesh and evil
Flooded his soul; our Lord stood there alone,
Bawling with anguish, trying to catch his breath,
The spiny hawthorns beside him fragrant with death.

John 11:34–37; 2 Samuel 15:30; Isaiah 53:4

229

THE RAISING OF LAZARUS [J]

They stood outside Lazarus's tomb,
A cave covered by a stone. "Roll it away!"
Said Jesus. Waiting beside him, Martha fumed.
"He stinks," she cried, "it's already been four days!"
The body now abandoned by its spirit,
Death worming its way into the dead man's flesh.
Martha needed once again to hear it,
"Now you will see the glory of God afresh";
Jesus looked up to the heavens and said,
"Thank you, Father, that you have heard my prayer."
And then he thundered his command to the dead,
"Lazarus, come forth!" His voice split the air,
Like the first day when his Father spoke:
Light shuddered into being, morning broke.

John 11:38–44; Genesis 1:1–4; Deuteronomy 33:27

230

THE RAISING Of LAZARUS [K]

Christ's voice shook the undercrofts of death—
The dead man waking from his last repose
Felt the cloth over his face, his breath
Pulling it into his nostrils as his lungs rose
In his chest, his limbs swaddled in linen strips,
The gagging stench of death all around.
Thirst heaved in his gullet up to his withered lips;
Glimmers of light drew him toward the sound
Of the voices of those in his final dream
Keening with grief above his fading sight.
Rising from habit, hearing his sisters scream,
He stumbled slowly out of his silent night.
"Unbind him; let him go," he heard him say,
Pushing him like a newborn into the day.

John 11:38–44; Job 13:28; Psalm 18:13–19

231

JESUS WITHDRAWS HIMSELf

Planning to kill a man who just has raised
Lazarus from the dead, do they understand
Nothing in their powers, in their words or ways,
Can defeat Jesus? Everyone in the land
Has heard the news, many of them believe—
This movement cannot be stopped. What can they do?
The heavy boot of Rome might press down and grieve
Many of their own. Caiaphas flew
Into a rage, Better one should die
Than many, a strange truth they could not bear
To hear, but for believers, the answer why
Our Savior came, to save us from despair
And gather up the many he has saved
To celebrate by dancing on our graves.

John 11:45–57; Amos 9:11–12; Revelation 21:4

232

JESUS PREDICTS HIS DEATH
FOR THE THIRD TIME

For the third time, Jesus tells the twelve
He will be handed over to the priests,
Condemned to death. Why does he have to tell
Them three times? They don't seem to have the least
Comprehension of this awful story.
Right after, they will argue about their place
In his cabinet, hoping he will give them glory
And elevate them. They jostle, make their case
As he describes his passion, his cross, his tomb
And resurrection. All for their miserable sakes.
They do not seem to sense that his ending looms.
The greatest sacrifice a man can make—
They squabble about rank as he goes to die.
He knows them all too well to wonder why.

Matthew 20:17–28; Acts 3:13; Acts 4:26–28

233

THE SON OF MAN CAME TO SERVE

Here two realities collide—our Lord
Speaks of the heavenly kingdom, out of time,
While the Zebedees build bureaucratic boards,
Ladders ambitious leaders struggle to climb
And get more power, command the normal perks
Of being with a company like his.
It baffled Jesus; did they get his work?
Hearing these men hoping to make the list
Of top managers, just after Jesus told
The disciples of his coming suffering and death,
How did they miss it? They lived in a world as old
As Babel, building a way to heaven by the flesh.
Christ turns the tables on them, a Lord who serves,
An unexpected changeup, a holy curve.

Matthew 20:20–28; Isaiah 51:22; Romans 8:16–17

234

THE BLIND MEN NEAR JERICHO

They sensed commotions all around and knew
Something was up. Hearing it was Christ,
They cried, "Have mercy on us," their volume grew,
"Son of David," they screeched and would not be quiet;
Those standing by tried to shut them up.
Jesus heard them bellering and asked,
"What do you want me to do?" His question stopped
Their cries. They turned toward his voice, rash
And urgent for his help. He pitied them
And touched their eyes; their sight broke open, shone
Into colors coming into focus; they saw him,
An ordinary man, like none they had known,
Filled with God, the fingers of his hands
Clearing a darkness drifting away like sand.

Matthew 20:29–34; Psalm 6:2; Acts 10:38

235

JESUS AND ZACCHAEUS

"Zacchaeus was a wee little man," we chant
To the small ones around us. I love to see their eyes
Widen to see the gestures of an old great aunt
Singing a song about a man their size.
They get it right. Zacchaeus, like a boy,
Runs to climb a tree to see the Lord.
"Zacchaeus, come down; I'm going to your house!" There's joy,
Good food, music, all he can afford.
The party overflows; Zacchaeus proves
A rich man can believe and make amends.
Christ has reordered all the tax man's loves,
Restored him as Abraham's son, and made a friend.
The eye of the needle widens; the gates of heaven
Open up, showing him all that he's been given.

Luke 19:1–10; Exodus 22:1–6; Leviticus 6:1–7

236

ANOINTING OF JESUS

Mary let down her hair to dry his feet.
Filling the house with fragrances of death,
His body not yet wrapped in winding sheets
Of linen binding his corpse without a breath,
Her waste is prodigal, misunderstood.
In a few days, this rehearsal will go live.
He will slide limply down the splintered wood;
His mother lamenting, he will not hear her cries.
They'll seal him away. They will not get to touch
His flesh or speak their fond farewells.
Judas sees figures, calculates how much
She spends to worship him. Jesus tells
The world her lavish gift cannot be sold,
His purse too small for all her love to hold.

John 12:1–8; Song of Songs 1:12; Acts 1:15–17

237

PALM SUNDAY

Son of David, they cry, throwing green palms
Down to mark his way. He rides a mule
Like Solomon into Jerusalem.
He knows the histories; he is no fool
Choosing a kingly mount to say, "I am
Ready to take my royal scepter up
On my way into town, healing the sick and lame,
Showing my kingdom's laws are love and hope.
I'll fill my house with those I have made fit
To enter the holy city. Paradise
Gleams at the end, through the grave and pit
Where I must battle the fiendish Lord of flies.
I ride into the realm where I will reign
After a war on a hill where I will be slain."

Matthew 21:1–11; 2 Samuel 5:6–10; 1 Kings 1:33

238

CURSING THE FIG TREE

The fig tree schools us in what it means to pray.
Jesus' lesson astonishes us all.
He shows how difficult the narrow way
Will be. How can our faith, which is so small,
Grow into a large tree, dispelling doubt?
Hyperboles of mountains crashing into seas
Dazzle us; we want to try it out,
Risking geographic catastrophes.
Testing God leads only to despair.
The fruit ends up barren, rusty husks.
Jesus wants to teach us the heart of prayer;
He plants in us the seeds of childlike trust.
Abandon all your doubt, and let him show
How much a tiny mustard seed can grow.

Matthew 21:18–22; Psalm 46:2–3; 2 Corinthians 9:10

239

THE SECOND TEMPLE CLEANSING [A]

Chaos throughout the city, pilgrims in town
For Passover. Lambs bleating, doves cooing,
Money changing hands, not a sound
Of prayer. Jesus has to keep on doing
His work, driving the thieves and robbers out,
Toppling the tables, letting the pigeons fly.
The prophets' words singing in his mouth
Seemed blasphemy for which he soon would die
Like the sacrificial animals being sold.
The temple, unclean as lepers he had healed,
Needed his cleansing in order to be whole.
His righteous anger means his fate is sealed
For throwing the money changers out of the square,
Restoring the temple to a house of prayer.

Matthew 21:12–17; Exodus 9:1–9; Zechariah 9:9

240

THE SECOND TEMPLE CLEANSING [B]

The temple cleansed, the lame and blind came in
To be healed, at the edge of what the law allows,
A children's choir adding to the din.
Filled with the frenzy of the Palm Sunday crowds,
"Hosanna to the Son of David!" they cry.
The clergy blow their stacks: "Don't you hear
Their blasphemy?" They could not abide
The worship of their young, making it clear
To Jesus who quotes Scripture back at them,
"Out of the mouths of babes will come God's praise,"
Bringing divisions to Jerusalem.
Shaking his head as they quibble over his phrase,
He turns on his heel, leaving to stay with his friends
In Bethany, death grinning around the bend.

Matthew 21:12–17; Psalm 8:2; Isaiah 56:7

241

fAITH TO MOVE MOUNTAINS

Jesus gets hungry on the way from Bethany
—didn't Martha feed him breakfast enough?
He sees up ahead a leafy fig tree
With not one fig growing. He does not touch
The tree to make figs appear. He curses it. It dies,
Withering at once. They cannot comprehend
How fast it happened, right before their eyes!
They marvel at his power. Could they be sent
The same? He starts talking faith and doubt,
Faith to move mountains to jump into lakes;
They will if your faith does not peter out.
It's what he says. Many have tried to take
His promise with a grain of salt instead
And eaten away the truth of what he said.

Matthew 21:18–20; Psalm 46:2; Hebrews 11:1

242

AUTHORITY OF JESUS QUESTIONED

Authority, they ask, who gives you power?
They think these questions will catch Jesus up,
Make him tell the secret of the hour
In the city. If he says God, ah! There's the rub:
Before they catch him in their toils, they're caught;
Once again, they learn Jesus is a master:
When he queries these leaders who they thought
John the Baptist was, they won't answer.
The first round goes to Jesus, a deadly game.
Admitting his powers are greater than any man,
They've lost the argument. Jesus' fame
Outrages them. Posit, if you can,
Whether you as teacher would have had the nerve
To judge the one you fear is the God you serve.

Matthew 21:23–27; Exodus 2:14; Acts 4:7

243

THE TWO SONS [A]

A parable that hardly needs a key,
Treating whether you live as you profess.
The first son says no, but later he will see
The truth and do what his Father asks, his protests
Ended. The younger son says he will but does not.
He speaks correctly and calls his father Lord
But fails to live his creed. Wars have been fought
Over writs of sacred papers that caused discord,
While the soldiers fighting and their generals lived
Lives that mocked the truths they killed to defend.
It matters what you do with what you believe.
Tax collectors and prostitutes at the end,
Having turned around and done their father's will,
Shall enter first the mansions Jesus builds.

Matthew 21:28–32; Proverbs 8:20–21; 2 Peter 2:21

244

THE TWO SONS [B]

Jesus knew small towns like the back of his hand.
As a little boy, he'd seen the swaggering drunk
Raving at the women he wanted on demand,
The tax collector stashing coins in his trunk;
He gave his life so they could turn around.
In a small town where I grew up, a pretty girl
Spent her life in bars; everyone in town
Knew what she did. Then Jesus changed her world.
Dazzled by Christ, joy in her weathered face,
She could not thank him enough. Each week she filled
Her John Deere pickup with stewing chickens, crates
Of eggs, fresh baked hot dish, gallons of milk
For others. I saw her last, sick unto death,
Blue heav'n about her, God shimmering on her breath.

Matthew 21:31–32; Luke 3:12; Colossians 3:12–17

245

THE WICKED TENANTS [A]

The landowner trusts his tenants and lets them work
Unsupervised. He's built the vineyard with care
And trusts their honor, certain they will not shirk
Their duties. At harvest, he sends his servants there
To get the fruit. The tenants beat and kill
The first, stoning another. They do this twice!
Then he says, "I will send my son! They will
Listen to him." But they plotted his demise,
Killing him for the land they could not afford.
There is no puzzle over what this story says,
But linger over this fond old foolish Lord
Trusting us with the only Son he has.
Electing to give us every chance, he knows
We're rotten to the core, as our fruitage shows.

Matthew 21:33–37; Psalm 80:8; Romans 8:1–8

246

THE WICKED TENANTS [B]

Echoes of Scripture sound in Jesus' words:
The tenants plot against him like Joseph's brothers,
And the son is killed outside the gate, but worst,
This is about us and not any others:
The son will die to save his killers. His will,
Written in blood on his testament,
Is sealed by his death, his last bequest fulfilled.
It was for us the Son of God was sent.
Hieronymus Bosch, the painter, depicts the scene:
Jesus, resolute, carrying his cross,
Crowded by those he's dying to save: vile, mean,
Ugly as sin, a savage picture of us.
Is that my face sniggering with glee,
Oblivious that his passion is for me?

Matthew 21:40–44; Genesis 37:12–28; Romans 5:6–11

247

THE WICKED TENANTS [C]

The scandal of our faith, a cornerstone
Despised, rejected, cast off by the mason, now
Set as the fundamental mark. It alone
Makes the entire building straight, allows
The builder to build higher, confident
It will never fall. From it, he finds the plumb
Justifying every stone against
Its angle of repose. His kingdom comes
Defying all the gravities of space,
Formed on foundations invisible but strong:
The baffling mysteries of heaven's grace.
God uses what our worldly wit thinks wrong;
He contradicts our measures. His design
Fashions a new dimension, a brand-new line.

Matthew 21:42–44; Psalm 118:22–23; 1 Corinthians 3:10–15

248

THE GREAT BANQUET [A]

God loves a party. The supper of the Lamb
Will last forever, the wedding of his son.
The list of guests, from us to Abraham,
Adam and Eve, Mary, goes on and on.
Servants deliver the summons everywhere,
But people get mad, refusing to be guests;
They have other duties and affairs,
So they kill the messengers, shunning the feast.
Angry, the Lord invites the good and bad,
Those who never thought to eat with kings.
Then by the thousands, they enter in, glad
And dressed to the nines with robes and diamond rings,
Trousseaus from the wardrobe of the Lord,
Worth a king's ransom only a prince could afford.

Matthew 22:1–10; 2 Samuel 9:1–13; Revelation 3:4–5

249

THE GREAT BANQUET [B]

To be dressed in the righteousness of Christ
Is necessary. You can't get through the gate
Without proper clothes; the sacrifice
Of Jesus on the cross will mediate
Between us, his blood the cover we need to live,
To take the fury of the Father's love.
To be with him, we need the dress he gives.
With, under, around, and through he proves
He cares for us. Without Christ, God's love is hell,
For he is a living fire. The lesson again
Is clear. He sent his Son to give himself
So everyone could safely enter in,
Be with him. On God's terms. The garment we wear
Will keep us near, as close as our suits can bear.

Matthew 22:11–14; Ephesians 4:17–24; Colossians 3:12–14

250

RENDER UNTO CAESAR

"Bring the coin you use to pay the tax!"
He said, more clever than any of the scribes.
One of them found the coin in his money bags.
They looked where the name of Caesar was inscribed,
Whose image none of them quite dared behold.
Christ cut the Gordian knot with the keenest blade:
"Render to Caesar the things that are Caesar's, to God
What is God's." They gasped at the wisdom he displayed.
His sentence echoed down the centuries.
This was the rule for Western governments:
The state for this world, the church eternity:
Two powers, two different realms. His answer sent
His inquisitors sheepishly away
Taxed by his brilliance, and what they had to pay.

Matthew 22:15–22; Romans 13:1–7; Hebrews 13:7

251

QUESTION OF SADDUCEES
REGARDING THE RESURRECTION

Seven brothers for one wife! An outrage!
Testing him on a belief they do not share,
Their question absurd on its very face.
Against the Lord, they haven't got a prayer.
He catches them on their ignorance of the word:
Marriage in heaven? A far from angelic thought.
Scripture wins the argument; have they not heard
God, the great I AM, is the living God,
Not ruler over the house of the dead
Where bones stretch out in a crypt beside their own,
Marrying away in darkness, head to head
With dusty death? Jesus breaks through the stone
Of their logic and raises up out of their graves
Abraham, Isaac, and Jacob, whom he has saved.

Matthew 22:23–33; Exodus 3:6; Deuteronomy 25:5–9

252

WHAT IS THE GREATEST COMMANDMENT?

Trying to trip up Jesus with questions is hard.
"Which is the greatest command?" right down his line:
"Love the Lord your God with all your heart,
With all your soul, and with all your mind
And your neighbor as yourself." Old words
All of us know enough to easily repeat.
To live them out, acting on what we've heard,
Giving all of one's self, each thought, each deed,
Over to the love of God is a kind of death.
Opening our hearts to our neighbor's souls
Changes us, turning our gaze from our own flesh
To others longing for God to make them whole,
All because our love for God has cleansed
Our hearts of the rubbish that blocks benevolence.

Matthew 22:34–40; Obadiah 1:15; 2 John 1:4–7

253

DAVID'S SON AND DAVID'S LORD

Jesus takes on the scribes with his family tree,
Confounding the scholars, hinting at the claims
About him, asking if the psalm says he
Is David's Son and David's Lord. He came
Into the world as Mary's son; his lines
Go back to David, into whose house he's born.
Also the Son of God, making him divine,
He is Messiah, therefore King David's Lord.
A cryptic passage the church has used a lot
To prove Jesus more than a prophet to them.
It silences skeptics and says that he is God,
The Lord of lords. Now in Jerusalem,
Jesus, our Lord, looks toward the cross, its pains
Chilling the blood running through his human veins.

Matthew 22:41–46; 2 Samuel 23:1–5; Psalm 110:1

254

WOES OF THE PHARISEES [A]

They disputed for hours, trying to trap
Jesus. He lashed out at them, clergy and scholars,
Splitting hairs and trying to expose gaps
In his logic; he stood in the temple square and hollered
Over their heads to his disciples and the crowds:
"Follow their words but not their deeds," he cried.
"They love their status; their station makes them proud.
They like processions, sycophants at their side,
Flaunting their titles, their place in the priestly ranks.
They elbow their ways proudly to the front,
Scarlet plumage hiding their beefy flanks.
Their lives contradict all they teach." The full brunt
Of his rage savaged the hypocrites he saw
Sitting in Moses's chair, throwing down the Law.

Matthew 23:1–7; Exodus 32:15–29; 1 Corinthians 1:18–25

255

WOES OF THE PHARISEES [B]

Hungry souls search for holiness,
Making long pilgrimages to find
A place where the secrets of the universe
Break through a crack in earth, all is aligned.
The gods come through, like hot lava bubbling
Up from the molten center of all things.
They wander for years, yearning and lost, troubling
Their spirits, straining to hear the old gods sing.
A young man yearning for God took such a trip—
Guitar, motorcycle, drugs, and girls—
Longing to stand on ecstasy's lip.
High in Machu Picchu, the top of the world,
He sang a hymn, then fell over laughing; the song
Said Christ had been traveling with him all along.

Matthew 23:13–15; Psalm 139:1–18; Romans 11:33–36

256

WOES OF THE PHARISEES [C]

To make death beautiful, we decorate
Coffins with flowers, covering stinking bones
Rotting inside, grinning skulls and pates,
Putrid, malodorous, graced by biblical stones.
This is what Jesus sees behind our facades:
Morticians trying to fancy up a corpse,
Hoping we might even deceive our God,
Trying to turn dead matter from its course,
Practicing to mimic a resurrected death,
Thinking to inhabit a whitened tomb.
Only a god can give these dry bones breath,
Raise them again as from their mother's womb.
Cry, God-a-mercy, give these old bones life;
Cut me from death with your dresser's knife.

Matthew 23:27–28; Ezekiel 13:10–11; Ezekiel 37:1–14

257

WIDOW'S MITE

Rich robed clergy processing to the box,
Dropping their ample coinage with rushing sounds.
Counterfeits. Jesus, watching the flocks
Of pilgrims in the women's court of the temple grounds,
Remarked on their display, their lack of faith.
Then he saw a poor widow who put
Two small coins in, hardly a pennyworth,
All that she had. Her deed showed the fruit
Of her trust that God would richly provide
All that she needed to live. She believed
In God's goodness and gave more than was advised.
Tightfisted with the gifts they had received,
They acted as if their small change was their own,
Mindless that all their deposits were hefty loans.

Luke 21:1–4; 2 Kings 12:9; Psalm 68:10

258

THE GRAIN OF WHEAT

A grain of wheat, alone, hard, and dry,
Is sterile unless it falls into the earth.
And, sodden with rain, rots and then it dies.
A burial, suddenly a second birth,
Raises it out of the ground, a tender shoot
Fragile and green. Water and sunshine fill
The growing leaf; soon, the golden fruit
Grown a hundredfold must be milled,
Ready to feed the hungry. So Jesus fed
The thousands, miracles of baskets brimming
With food, manna from heaven, living bread
To nourish us forever. The seed springing
Into words, his promises our daily meal
That now his final testament reveals.

John 12:23–26; 1 Corinthians 15:36–38; 2 Corinthians 9:10

259

JESUS' MINISTRY AND ITS RESULTS

Jesus cries out so all the world can hear
He is his Father's word for all the earth
Sent to speak and bring the Father near
To us, the reason for his human birth:
To be the light dispelling all the dark.
He came not to judge but came to save,
But his words ripen into judgments that mark
Our lives for good. From the beginning, he was made
For us; we were a gleam in the Father's eye
When the Spirit hovered over the primordial waters,
Bringing the formless void into life,
Born in a breath, a world of sons and daughters.
Blooming with light, he goes to the darkest space
To guide us back into his mansioned place.

John 12:37–50; John 1:1–17; Genesis 1:1–5

260

JESUS LEAVES THE TEMPLE

When Jesus leaves the temple, he forecasts
Terrible times, seeing ahead to the end,
Not one stone left on another. The past
Is over; we hear what all the signs portend,
Giving us pictures we see in every war:
Orphans weeping in the rubbled street,
Women picking through rubbish near and far
For food to feed the children under their feet,
No one to cherish, no one to keep the faith.
The temple will perish, but Jesus will build up
A temple of his body raised from death
After he has drunk its bitter cup,
A temple like Eden, which God would gladly fill.
Happy for company, a home Christ goes to build.

Matthew 24:1–31; 1 Kings 9:7–9; 2 Thessalonians 2:2–6

261

SECOND COMING PROPHECY

Leaving the temple behind, Jesus walked
Up to the Mount of Olives to watch the crowds
Filling the vast courtyards. As they talked,
Marveling at the huge stones, the massive grounds,
Larger than any edifice in the world,
Herod's offering, Jesus warned it would fall,
All its leavings scattered rubble. His words
Terrified them, nothing left of the walls,
"False prophets will come, mislead you, false Christs."
Jesus spoke clearly to all of them.
"Wars and rumors of wars, nations rise
Against nation." They sat above Jerusalem
Hearing of tribulations, labor pains,
A temple to be raised from our Lord's remains.

Matthew 24:3–14; Daniel 9:16; Malachi 3:2–4

262

THE BUDDING FIG TREE

Learn to read the signs of the end of time
Like you mark the coming of summer in a tree:
The branch greens up as the sap begins to climb
Up from the roots. Everyone knows they will see
Budding and later fruit. The growth is clear.
And when the Son of Man returns, the signs
Are tribulations rising as he nears.
The sun will go dark, the moon no longer shine,
Stars fall from the heavens. All the earth will mourn.
He will appear on the clouds; a loud trumpet call
Will gather the elect from the four winds, the heavens torn,
Too late to change our worldly ways and fall
To our knees repenting. Now what we know
Is that turmoil continues, his coming slow.

Matthew 24:32–35; Daniel 7:13–14; Revelation 7:13–14

263

THE TEN BRIDESMAIDS

Ten bridesmaids, five were foolish, five were wise,
Young women waiting for the bridegroom to come,
Eager to party. At midnight comes the cry.
The bridegroom is near, ready to take them home.
They trim their lamps and go to meet him; the feast
Will soon begin. The foolish have used up their oil;
They are not prepared, not in the least;
The wise need all their oil or the night will be spoiled.
The foolish run to town for some; they return
And knock on the bridegroom's door; it opens to light.
He does not know them; their lamps flicker and burn.
They are left outside in the clutches of night.
It is too late; they get no second chance.
They wail outside the music, the wedding dance.

Matthew 25:1–13; 1 Thessalonians 4:16–18; 2 Timothy 2:19

264

THE TALENTS [A]

A sober teaching—the boss leaves his living
To servants and goes away. They do not know
Where he is going, how long; he's gone without giving
Any instructions. What are they to do?
The first two get busy and double their returns;
The third does nothing, stashing the cash away.
Risking nothing, there's nothing he can earn.
When his master comes back, he has much to say:
"I knew you were a hard man, Lord," he faults
The boss, like Adam in the garden pointing at Eve,
Even accusing him of sin; it is the fall
Happening all over again. What he believes
Accuses him. The master will hear no more;
Weary of his glibness, he shows him the door.

Matthew 25:14–30; Genesis 3:12; Romans 12:9–13

265

THE TALENTS [B]

We know the type: the rich who think they're poor,
Giving little away, hoarding their wealth,
Doing nothing for their gracious Lord.
Pleading poverty or failing health,
They speak piously at meetings to show
Their heart is really in the proper place,
Though their charities are scarce. Who knows
Their pledges, their numbers, or their state of grace?
Making cases for why they will not give.
They disapprove of the way they were asked,
Critical of how those raising money live.
They put on righteousness, a pious mask,
Religious reasons for not giving a dime;
They'll not run out of money but out of time.

Matthew 25:14–30; 1 Corinthians 16:1–4; 1 Timothy 6:17–19

THE SHEEP AND THE GOATS [A]

A great hubbub of activity
Swirls around as Jesus separates
The sheep from the goats. In the Sistine Chapel, we see
Its finality. The faces show their fate:
Joy in those rising to heaven, others going down
Holding their hands over their eyes and sunk
In hellish despair, their bodies drifting around,
Their eyes filled with horror, for they have drunk
Deeply of damnation. Bartholomew
With the face of the painter dangling in air,
A furious masterpiece against the blue;
Its powers arrest and make us stop and stare:
Jesus has come to judge the quick and the dead,
Standing there, making good on all he said.

Matthew 25:31–46; Joel 3:12; Hebrews 13:1–2

267

THE SHEEP AND THE GOATS [B]

"When did we see you?" Neither of them know,
Not those who helped their neighbor or those who did not.
Do they only recognize him in a long robe
From a medieval painting with an old god
Peering like a grandpa from the sky blue heavens?
Trying to feed God or give him clothes is absurd.
Jesus inhabits us to see we are given
What we need to live. Deep in our flesh, his word
Makes us all holy. He shows us how
Loving our neighbor is to cherish him.
He wants our worship simple, kneeling down
To the naked, the hungry, prisoners, all of them.
He hides himself in us so we might see
Incarnate love, its plain simplicity.

Matthew 25:31–46; Proverbs 14:31; 1 Corinthians 8:12

268

JESUS' LAST PROPHECY OF HIS DEATH

In two days, Jesus says, the Son of Man
Will be handed over to be crucified.
God is delivering him up; it is the plan.
As God the Father sends his Son to die,
The great drama of the universe
Is in its final act. The Passover Lamb
Will be sacrificed at our hands, the silver purse
Will be filled, and this son of Abraham
Will be the ram in the thicket to take our place.
God gives him over and lets us do the deed;
We will behold the terror of his grace
When we see the thorns and watch Christ Jesus bleed,
Taking into his wounds all the pain
Of those pounding the spikes, their hate in vain.

Matthew 26:1–5; Ezra 6:20–21; Psalm 2:2

269

BARGAIN OF JUDAS

The fragrant ointment filled the room with love;
A year's wages, Judas reckoned, being spent
Anointing Jesus. It was more than enough.
In a rage, Judas, who felt deceived, went
To the chief priests to ask how much they'd pay
For him to hand over the Lord to them.
A mere pittance of cash to betray
Jesus. Nothing like what she'd wasted on him.
Worshipped by his followers and women of wealth,
He was losing his purpose, letting the rebels down.
Judas felt vindicated in his stealth;
Jesus was an impostor, he had found.
Now he had to wait, watching for a chance,
Avoiding like sin Christ's penetrating glance.

Matthew 26:14–16; Proverbs 26:24–28; Isaiah 1:22

270

THE PREPARATION OF THE PASSOVER

"Ask a man carrying a water jar
Where we will hold the Passover meal tonight,"
Jesus told them. Thousands from afar
Filling the city to celebrate the rite;
A man doing women's work on a festive day
They would find quickly, hidden in this sign
Out in the open, waiting to show the way
Where the twelve could be together and safely dine,
Away from suspicious clergy and Roman swords.
Eager to enjoy the ritual meal
In the real presence of their wondrous Lord
But fearing what this dinner might reveal,
Pondering whether his prophecies were true,
Waiting for his words to fall like silver dew.

Mark 14:12–16; Exodus 12:18; 1 Corinthians 5:7

271

INSTITUTION OF THE LORD'S SUPPER

Remembering Moses and the exodus,
The blood of the Lamb on the lintels meant to save
Those under its sign, Christ gives to us
Bread, broken and blessed, his body that he gave
For us to eat, manna so we can live
Forever. We drink his blood, his testament
To us, a legacy of life he gives
So death will pass over us, a death he spent
To pay our debt; for this, he had to die
Knowing that with his body, he could free
Captives to sin and death and satisfy
Our longings, handing over eternity
For us to chew on as we hear his will,
Wondering as Satan sifts us in his mill.

Matthew 26:26–29; Zechariah 9:11; Luke 22:31–32

272

THE SAVIOR WASHES THE DISCIPLES' FEET

Christ rising from the table to wash their feet
Baffled them, seeing the Son of David bend
Like a worshipper before the mercy seat
Bowing to them. For this, our Lord was sent,
Kneeling to serve us, to make us clean.
Unseemly, Peter cries, this is not right.
He wants what humility cannot receive.
Then Jesus washes him in floods of light.
"Oh, cleanse me, Lord," he cries with all of us.
"Come, rid me of my darkness, make me new,
A different person, diamond out of dust,
Sparkling inside the water, fresh as dew."
O Jesus, help us trust your kneeling here
To worship us with acts of simple cheer.

John 13:21–30; Genesis 18:4–5; 1 John 1:8–10

273

JUDAS LEAVES THE UPPER ROOM

A morsel of bread from Jesus' hand
Dipped in the cup, then Satan entered in.
For him, a witch's Sabbath with a bad end
For Judas who took and ate and swallowed sin.
Thirty pieces of silver to betray
Our Lord. In, with, and under Satan moved
Into the man, a parody of grace,
A Eucharist of hate from perfect love.
He ran into the night toward the court,
Silver gleaming like a moon that drew
The tides of hatred slithering out of his heart.
His own Lord, the vintner of a vicious brew.
The forces of the universe at war,
The devil's viceroy slinking out the door.

John 13:21–30; Luke 22:3–6; Psalm 41:9

Jesus' Farewell Discourses

274

THE GLORY OF JESUS' DEATH

Judas disappears into the night,
And Jesus calls it glory. It seems odd;
Our natural wisdom trembles at Judas's flight
As evil marshals its troops against our God.
The Son of Man looks ahead. Now begins
The glorious battle between light and dark.
God stooping down into the fray to win,
Facing the cross and grave, making his mark
As God's word in person. What looks like defeat
Is victory: his death will be the death
Of death, undoing chaos; Look! Christ will beat
The devil at his own game. We catch our breath
To see the cosmic forces lining up
And Jesus draining the dregs of Judas's cup.

John 13:31–32; Mark 14:17–21; Psalm 115:4–8

275

WHERE THE DISCIPLES CANNOT GO

Jesus is going where we cannot come,
At least for now, although we seek to go.
Abiding with us, making his home with us.
Reclining, he speaks of what we do not know,
His hands lining out invisible shapes. Flesh
Cannot endure the fire of God or grace
Unmediated; we need something to protect
Our bodies from divinity, a place
Habitable as Eden, a garden filled
With foods delectable, where we can dine.
There in the paradise he goes to build;
Sanctified, we can drink his wine,
Hearing the waters burble as they reveal
All of the love that brought us to this meal.

John 13:33; Deuteronomy 4:24; Hebrews 12:28–29

276

LOVE ONE ANOTHER

To love one another is Christ's new command.
He looks around the dark room at each one,
Torches flickering, trying to understand
His word, unable to do what he has done,
Dying and rising. The waters flow from his well;
His love is the love we are to bring
To others, not what bubbles up in ourselves.
It surges from him like a mountain spring,
Out of his body into ours. It never goes dry.
We pass it on. Mother Teresa served
The poor, filling their cups from his well, a rich supply,
But never once in all that time had heard
A word from God. She took what Christ had given,
Passing it on with a daily sip from heaven.

John 13:34–35; John 4:13–15; John 7:37–38

277

PETER'S OVERCONFIDENCE

Peter again covers his eyes with his hands.
He groans, shielding his face from the candlelight.
He wants to go with him, do something grand
For Jesus, even laying down his life,
Anything to prove his love for the Lord.
What good will that do? Jesus has to give
His life and be raised from the dead. Christ's word
Rebukes Peter for his bluster. He believes
He is stronger than he is. Christ prophesies
He will deny him three times the next day
Before the rooster crows. The one who must die
Is Jesus. He is the one who will have his say.
Peter will deny what he has said,
His cockiness and swagger slain instead.

John 13:36–38; Matthew 26:33–35; 2 Peter 1:13–15

278

JESUS PROMISES TO RETURN
AND TAKE US TO THE FATHER

Jesus comforts us, for he is God.
He will come back and take us to himself.
For a little while, our master will be gone
Preparing a home for us like nothing else.
Mansions, he says, in his Father's place
Filled with many rooms, not like a dorm
But spacious dwellings to abide in, graced
By conversation, music, lovely forms,
Beauties the eye has never seen, with sounds
The ear has never heard nor words that tell
What he will fit us for. Faith is the ground
We stand on waiting to see where we will dwell.
His absence occupies us; we believe
He will return again and never leave.

John 14:1–3; John 16:22; 1 Peter 3:14–17

279

I AM THE WAY, THE TRUTH, THE LIFE

The way, the truth, the life; no one will come
Into the Father's presence by another way.
Sometimes my own prelate, I dissent from
This view, arguing with its premise to say
I want another route, a sliding door
Over the threshold mortals cannot cross.
I would blaze my own trail, be my own Lord.
He made himself the way at great cost,
Spending himself to break the barriers down,
To open up the universe, prepare
Celestial repasts, gold and silver crowns.
Our wills rebel against him; do we care?
Without change, I am priest of my own faith
Lost in my own heaven, a circle of death.

John 14:4–6; Hebrews 10:19–22; 1 John 5:20

280

TO SEE THE FATHER

"If you have seen me, you have seen the Father."
Philip asks our question, "Show us, then!"
All the powers of language must be gathered
To demonstrate what he is telling them.
More than the spitting image of his dad,
He and his Father are of one being, the same,
But we see Jesus, mortal like us and glad
He lived on earth among us. Because he came,
We behold God inhabiting our flesh.
For God is a consuming fire, pure love,
Who needed cover to be with us; in a crèche,
Jesus was born to live as flesh and blood
So we could know God as he is and see
Love pulsing through the cosmos for you and me.

John 14:7–11; Hebrews 12:28–29; 1 John 2:13

281

JESUS GIVES LIFE TO HIS DISCIPLES

Christ will do great things through us, he says.
Even more than he did in his own time.
Reclining there, can they imagine the ways
They will travel the world from Palestine,
Suffering mocking, flogging, imprisonment,
Destitute, mistreated, filled with need—
From the earliest, these poor apostles went
Everywhere to bring his word, their deeds
Binding up wounds, bread for the poor, good news
For millions dying to hear he lives in us.
He sends us to bear witness to the truth,
Loves us enough to die upon a cross.
Now he calls us to extend his reach—
When we do his bidding, our works preach.

John 14:12–14; Matthew 28:18–20; Hebrews 11:32–40

282

JESUS PROMISES HIS DISCIPLES
THE COMFORTER

When we love someone, we are glad to do
Their bidding and nourish our bonds. Jesus tells
The disciples, "My Father will send to you
A Helper, an Advocate, who will dwell
With you." They look around. Is this Helper here?
"I am with you when you worship me."
Jesus is teaching them, trying to make clear
His Spirit is with us, one we cannot see
But know it is the love we share for him
Beyond all measurement; they sense it move
Like a soft breeze fluttering among them,
Whispering the truth, evidence of his love,
Standing beside them while their Lord is gone,
Working with joy to make his presence known.

John 14:15–17; Romans 8:9–11; 1 Corinthians 2:14–16

283

JESUS PROMISES NOT TO
LEAVE THEM ORPHANS

As he speaks, he watches their faces turning glum.
His long speeches reassuring them
They would not be orphans, that he would come
Again, puzzle them. They needed him,
His physical presence, the comfort of their Lord.
Poetry to say he would be gone
A little while. Why all these matchless words?
He has to die so his mission will get done.
He contradicts all reason; the dead raised up,
It topples convention; How can they believe
He lives so they will live? A foolish hope
They've never seen before. Of course, they grieve.
He speaks of something far beyond their ken;
Things will be better and never the same again.

John 14:18–20; Romans 5:10; 1 John 2:24–25

284

JESUS PROMISES THE DISCIPLES
HE WILL DWELL WITH THEM

Good Judas asks, "Lord, how will you reveal
Yourself to us?" A candle flares in the depths
Of the room as they look at each other. We feel
It in the picture he paints, how close we're kept:
Loving us so we can learn to love,
Keeping his commands to his delight,
The Father and the Counselor move
Into our hearts, tabernacling with us, his light
Glowing in us, the temple where he dwells.
Homeschooling, teaching us the truths he bore.
The tutor, the Holy Spirit, there to tell
Mysteries beating at the very core
Of the universe dancing with joy to show
Their pleasure in our studies with the one they know.

John 14:21–26; Exodus 29:45; 1 John 2:26–27

285

JESUS GIVES HIS DISCIPLES HIS PEACE

Jesus sees the end when the ruler of the world
Appears. "Let not your hearts be troubled, peace,
I give you, peace," he says. A few more words,
"Your pain and suffering may never cease
In this age. My peace will give you confidence.
With it, you can face the devil's might.
You will see me suffer, my garments rent,
The noon go darker than the darkest night—
I do my Father's will. Be not afraid.
My peace, past understanding, will calm your hearts.
Facing the fiercest torture, you will be made
Strong enough to pass through the darkest parts."
Dietrich Bonhoeffer went to his death
Calmly, filled with Christ's peace. It comes with faith.

John 14:27–31; Ephesians 2:17–22; Philippians 2:5–7

286

I AM THE VINE

The root of all, the source of all that lives.
Through him comes life, all the food we need
Coursing through our arteries to give
Life to our spirits, bodies, fruit, and seed.
His words cleanse the lines to make a place
Where he abides, and we abide with him,
A home, comfortable and filled with grace,
Where the juices fructify the limbs.
Without their cleansing, the branches wither and die;
The gardener throws them into the fire to burn.
Even tender shoots he prunes away
For richer harvests; helping us to learn,
The Father readies this house to dwell with us,
A nursery of grace that he will tend with love.

John 15:1–8; Romans 11:22–24; Revelation 3:20

287

JESUS CALLS US FRIENDS

No longer servants, now he calls us friends,
The source supplying us with the living vine
Straight from the heart of God where all time ends—
Eternity—a guest who comes to dine,
A god who spends himself to live with us,
To sacrifice his life for company.
He came from silence into speech we trust
To show us love, physical and sweet,
The pleasure of someone's skin against our own,
A feast of tasty gifts of wine and bread,
Vistas of beauty he made for us alone,
Given so our bodies and spirits can be fed.
He is the guest and host we feed upon
Sent from the Father's bosom, his only Son.

John 15:9–17; Matthew 12:46–50; 2 John 1:8

288

JESUS TEACHES HIS DISCIPLES THEY WILL BE HATED

The demons knew him at once and wildly shrieked
Against his very being. Clerical powers
Sensed Jesus was dangerous. They would speak
Against him, fearing rightly his movement would flower
Into rebellion. The world hates the ones
Who have set their roots deep into the Lord,
Grafted into him, feeling his juices run
In their veins. These vitals cannot be ignored:
Jesus dwelling in us works a change:
He feeds us food the world cannot abide,
Elixirs against death that make us strange
To the world; His body keeps us well supplied
To stand against the dark, demonic hate
From worldlings who by nature loathe his traits.

John 15:18–21; 1 Corinthians 4:11–13; James 4:4

289

JESUS TELLS THE DISCIPLES
THE WORLD HATES THEM

Tough truths from our Savior: worldlings detest
Christians, the church, Scriptures, even God.
The Psalmist marked it too. We see it best
Watching Christ's presence stir the devil's pot,
Roiling up pogroms, gulags, labor camps.
Solzhenitsyn saw in his captor's face
The wolf's teeth, the heavy-booted tramp
Of feet, the fury against a scrap of grace,
Reading in the eyes of his jailer the surety
His theory should rid the world of Christ.
All are capable of cruelty,
Solzhenitsyn believed Christ's sacrifice
Served for the guard as much as for himself,
His own bent for terror needing to be spelled.

John 15:22–25; Psalm 69:4; 1 Thessalonians 2:14–16

290

JESUS PROMISES HIS DISCIPLES THE SPIRIT'S WITNESS IN THE WORLD

The Spirit of Truth, the Counselor, Christ sends
As witness to him to teach his mysteries
From eternity; the Helper tends
God's work and vivifies all that is his.
He interprets and opens up the word
And helps us fathom what our Lord has done
So we can speak of all we have seen and heard,
Teaching us how to preach of God's own Son.
The Spirit comes to demonstrate the way
Jesus comes from the Father. He sends us forth
To tell others all that he has to say.
It's how the good news spread over the earth.
Hudson Taylor caught the passion to bring
The Gospel to China, changing everything.

John 15:26–27; Acts 4:8; 3 John 1:12

291

JESUS PREPARES HIS DISCIPLES
FOR THE WORLD'S HATE

Jesus warns us of all that lies ahead:
Separations, persecutions, pain
Caused by fanatics who want their critics dead.
To kill convictions, people must be slain.
Tyrants snuff out ideas they reject
By wanton terror. None of us should doubt
That we will suffer for our faith. Inspect
The human heart, all darkness, undevout,
Idolatrous, doing evil to be good,
Using the stake to keep a dogma pure.
Our history burns with monsters who understood
Only capricious violence assured
Their doctrines: many the despots, scholars, popes
Who lit bonfires hoping to extinguish hope.

John 16:1–4a; Acts 8:1–3; 2 Corinthians 4:7–12

292

HOW THE PARACLETE WORKS

By the flickering light, the terror has begun.
Jesus knows the disciples are depressed.
His talk of coming and going and being gone
Brings them a sorrow they cannot express.
They will see horrors plunging them into grief
As he trudges his way out to the cross and grave.
They will lose him, a defeat, they still believe,
A loss they cannot vanquish by being brave.
Here is the crux, the irony of faith:
He has to leave to send his Spirit here.
If he were simply flesh, his image would fade.
The Spirit brings him to life, and he appears:
Raising Christ to dwell within our hearts,
Building a temple from each troubled part.

John 16:4b–7; John 14:26; Acts 2:32–33

293

THE PARACLETE SHOWS US THE TRUTH

All that the flesh believes is upside down.
Unbelief keeps us from seeing through
The shades of unrighteousness circling around.
The Spirit, the Helper, demonstrates the truth,
Revealing the structure of the galaxies,
Teaching that Christ is Lord, giving us faith;
We will not see him but know that all is his;
The ruler of this world will meet his fate.
In a few hours, Jesus will have died.
Friends will remove him to a virgin tomb;
Soldiers will watch—he will be sealed inside—
Nothing from the torn curtain pierces the gloom—
Then in a bolt of lightning, he will be raised:
Death will be dead and Satan's powers slain.

John 16:8–11; 1 Corinthians 12:3; 1 Peter 1:3–9

294

THE PARACLETE LEADS THE CHURCH BY THE TRUTH

The Spirit he is sending will make his face
Brighter than any sun they've seen themselves.
His brilliance will dazzle them, light with grace.
Later, they will understand him well.
He helps them learn, chastening their thoughts
Like the sun blotting out all other lights.
The Helper discloses more of Christ and God
So Jesus only will be glorified.
We sit in church and hear the preacher preach,
A word takes fancy in us, we wander off
And dream of dinner, or suddenly our visions reach
Into the truth; we see through mundane stuff,
Christ dawning before us, something we heard,
The glory of God before us from airy words.

John 16:12–15; Psalm 25:5; Hebrews 10:19–25

295

JESUS GIVES HIS DISCIPLES THE JOYS OF HIS RESURRECTION, HIS RETURN, AND THEIR ANSWERED PRAYERS

A little while, he says, and you will grieve,
And then in a little while, you will rejoice,
Like a woman giving birth. She cries and weeps
With fear and dread, then hearing the baby's voice
For the first time, she forgets the pain,
The infant gurgling at her swollen breast.
So after the horror of these next three days,
Morning will break, gladness will be your dress.
These will be birth pangs, like someone being born,
A man tearing through death, himself again,
Miracles the flesh has never known before.
You will have witnessed something beyond your ken:
Sorrow has sown its seeds in tears, but look!
Now with laughter, we'll harvest the grief we brooked.

John 16:16–24; Psalm 126; Isaiah 26:17–18

296

JESUS GIVES HIS DISCIPLES BETTER KNOWLEDGE OF THE FATHER, THEMSELVES, AND HIS RELATIONS TO THEM

This is enough to break our Savior's heart.
They look puzzled, the light seems to dawn.
"At last," they say, "we know who you are:
You come from God." But where he will be gone
They have no clue. He is certain they will flee
Into the darkness, fearful they will be killed.
He comforts them and gives them all his peace,
Knowing they are unbelievers still.
The pathos here: our Savior sees ahead,
That he must face the devil all alone,
That all their empty promises are dead,
Buried beneath their heavy hearts of stone.
They will take refuge in the peace he gives
Even if their disbelief is all that lives.

John 16:25–33; Isaiah 63:5; Ephesians 2:14–16

297

JESUS PRAYS FOR HIS AND HIS FATHER'S GLORY

The Father, alone able to give life,
Sends Christ to give eternal life to all
As Jesus prays, looking forward to the strife
He must suffer: the vinegar, the gall,
To be raised up, ascending for each of us,
Building his home in us, being our food
And drink, a finished vintage from the cross,
Hints of great passion from its rough-hewn wood.
Images of pearl with rich bouquets
Blossom in new aromas we will see
As we listen to their fresh dimensions play
In our new bodies by the crystal stream.
God will be present with us, forever young,
His glories dazzling, Father and the Son.

John 17:1–5; Jeremiah 10:10–11; 1 John 2:25

298

SANCTIƒY THEM IN ΥOUR TRUTH, ΥOUR WORD IS TRUTH

These are your words, sanctify them in your truth:
Deep words from Jesus the pastor would repeat
After the Gospel text was read. From our youth,
Our pastors prayed them before they'd start to preach.
"Heavenly Father, your word is truth," they said,
Believing truth crowded sin from the heart,
Bringing sin, death, and the devil to their death.
Christ makes us holy, filling us, every part.
As he was dying, our old pastor opened up
The Scriptures to his nurse. She watched his eyes
Gleaming with holiness, observing his hope
Shine through his translucent skin as he died
Glowing with light as he left his bag of worms,
New life beginning for him on Jesus' terms.

John 17:6–19; 2 Samuel 7:28; 1 Peter 1:3–5

299

JESUS PRAYS FOR THE CHURCH

Using marriage as a sign we are one—
As Christ is in the Father, we are in him,
His bride, together, all brighter than the sun,
Like garlands of sweet flowers or precious gems.
Divinity is in us; our wedding dance
Circles the bright empyrean for joy
With miracles of wine, his mother's glance
Beaming over the angels to see her boy.
Forgotten all our human pains and hurts,
Each one known to the highest heaven.
His grief for us filling the universe
Now washed away by the blood the Son has given.
Even in the flesh, we fathom what will be
Celebrating our nuptials through all eternity.

John 17:20–26; Romans 12:5; Galatians 3:28

The Way to the Cross

300

GETHSEMANE

After singing a hymn of praise, they left
The room, crossing the Kidron, a turbid brook.
David leaped over it, fleeing, bereft
And weeping, fearing Absalom. It shook
The city with terror. Now David's Son climbs
The Mount of Olives, the glory of the Lord
Ascending to betrayal, ashes of crimes
Against his Father floating in a spring of words.
Toward the garden our Savior makes his way.
Soon, his disciples will abandon him
Even as he falls on his face to weep and pray.
While they sleep, he will sweat tears of blood for them.
Knowing this all, he leads them through the dark
Into the haven where evil will make its mark.

John 18:1; 2 Samuel 15:13–23; 2 Kings 15:9–13

301

THE GARDEN

Jesus went to the garden to restore
Eden, the world lost by Adam and Eve
Driven out by the angel's flaming sword.
Now Jesus enters it, Gethsemane,
The olive press, which crushed olives for oil.
Jesus will fling himself against the ground
Where the old, ancient serpent hisses and coils.
We see grief pressing the Savior down,
Shuddering with terror as he prays,
"Father, if you will, remove this cup,
Not my will but yours." He will obey.
Sorrowful, he goes to wake them up,
The serpent slithering in the darkness to strike
The Son of God and Adam, the world's true light.

John 18:1–2; Genesis 3:1–8; Psalm 74:14

302

THE DISCIPLES FALL ASLEEP

They saw him once on a mountain glorified,
Peter, James, and John. He asked them to watch
With him through creation's darkest night,
Evil besmirching everything they touched.
All of his farewell talk had bothered them.
Weary with all the mysteries they'd heard,
They lay down thinking to comfort him,
Trying to sort out the Savior's final words.
Their eyes grew heavy; they fell into deep sleep.
Three times Jesus rose up in the dark
To find himself alone in his hour of need.
All three lost in their dreams, the Savior's heart
Breaking to find mere flesh of little help;
An angel ministered to him, no one else.

Matthew 26:40–44; Luke 22:39–46; 1 Peter 4:7

303

JESUS UPBRAIDS HIS DISCIPLES

The sleeping James and John once had vowed
That they could drink the cup that now our Lord
Prays to avoid. Soon, they will see him bowed
Under the weight of the sins of all the world
Poured into the chalice that he agreed to drink.
There in the garden, sweating bloody tears,
He knows that he stands at the very brink
Of history. Here is the sum of all our fears.
Nothing we can do but fall into the deepest sleep
While Jesus sobs, alone, tasting the earth.
We could not give him solace nor even weep
Repentant tears, our slumbers showing our worst,
For as he goes to die, we fall away
Despite our promise lying in a green shade.

Matthew 26:40–44; Psalm 43:5; Hebrews 5:7–9

304

THE LIGHT OF THE WORLD MEETS LIGHTS OF THE WORLD

Off in the distance, they see flickering lights
Moving slowly toward them; now is the hour!
Hundreds of soldiers, priests, and their acolytes
Led by Judas into Eden's bower.
Lanterns and torches showing the way, their swords
Glinting beside them as they halt their march.
Jesus steps forward: "Whom are you looking for?"
"Jesus of Nazareth," they shout from the dark.
They hear the Master answer, "I AM he!"
The name topples them over, onto the ground,
Felled by forces their spies could never see,
Two worlds colliding, one Judas had not found.
Their lights cannot outshine the Light of the World,
A glimpse they could not catch gleaming in his word.

John 18:3–6; Exodus 3:13–18; Revelation 1:17–18

305

THE KISS OF JUDAS

The traitor moves toward Jesus to give him a kiss.
No night darker than Judas's soul this night,
We can hear his disappointments hiss
As the Son of Man, surrounded by Roman might,
Greets Judas kindly, calling him his friend.
The garden a place for prayer and quiet talk,
Jesus betrayed in a shade of innocence,
Like Eden, where in the evening, God would walk.
The wily serpent comes again to bring
Dissension. He will be undone when he sets his fangs
Into Jesus, suffering his own medicine
For his dirty work; he will die of deadly pangs,
Birthing his chaos in a lovely space,
Kissing our Lord on his kind and tear-stained face.

Matthew 26:47–50; Psalm 41:5–13; John 13:18

306

PETER DRAWS HIS SWORD /
HEALING THE EAR OF THE SERVANT

Peter draws his sword out of its sheath
To strike Malchus, cutting off his ear.
Brave but foolish, he could have caused the death
Of hundreds, sparking the melee Pilate feared.
"Put back your sword. I must drink the cup;
This is neither the time nor place for swords."
His hour has come. Nothing may interrupt
The drama. He touches the ear; it is restored.
Merciful until the bloody end,
Jesus must suffer and die on the cross.
To conquer Satan, he cannot relent.
The cup brimming with terror must be drunk for us.
Swords have no power to vanquish the evil one
Nor further the kingdom of God's only Son.

John 18:10–11; Isaiah 51:22–23; Psalm 44:6

307

ARREST OF JESUS

With thick cords, they bind him, but he commands,
"Let my people go!" With Moses's words,
He frees them as soldiers tie his gentle hands.
His voice they follow; was it God they heard?
Although he lets them bind him, he is in charge.
Even if they think they have the power,
His forces are the angels, their number large.
Submitting to the devil at this hour
Looks like weakness, but it will show his strength.
It confounds rulers who number up their swords.
Calculating kingdoms, their breadth and length,
But cannot take the measure of this captive Lord
Able to loose his bonds as he is bound,
To love his betrayer as their metal sounds.

John 18:8; Matthew 26:45–49; Daniel 7:10

308

CHRIST SPEAKS TO THE CROWD

Onlookers gathered around to witness the scene.
Bound, he spoke into the dark to them,
Marveling at their curiosity,
Braving the Passover crowds of Jerusalem
To catch a glimpse of the moment. The past three years
He had sat teaching freely in the temple,
Men jostling each other to better hear.
His authority seemed clear and simple,
Speaking as one who had written the law.
The rich robed clergy, always in the know,
Were shocked, debating with him to find his flaws.
The prophets had prophesied this long ago.
The disciples fled, fearing they would be killed,
As Jesus saw Scripture's word fulfilled.

Matthew 26:55–56; Psalm 88:8; John 16:32

309

THE FLIGHT OF THE DISCIPLES

They fled into the night, fearful, afraid,
As he had prophesied. All alone,
They left him after they saw him being betrayed,
Running in terror over the cobblestones
Into the darkness, mixing in with the crowds,
Safe for the moment, hiding with family or friends
Whispering over the meal, curtains like shrouds
Over the windows. Here we see again
We are no earthly good for Jesus' work.
Only he can kill the devil off,
Beat sin and death so they no longer lurk
In the shadows, waiting for us, ready to scoff
At our efforts. The only thing that can be done:
Hide in the scarlet robes of God's own Son.

Matthew 26:56; Isaiah 53:3; Psalm 109:25

310

THE SANHEDRIN TRIAL OF JESUS

Insurrection bubbled in the crowds
Milling around the city. The high priest
Caiaphas feared open rebellion. The proud
Prelate had once surmised it was at least
Better that one die for many instead
Of a bloodbath. He spoke more clearly then he knew.
In a phrase, he captured what the Gospel says,
"God sent his Son, one for all," this was true.
The guilty masses of humanity
Can only be redeemed by one who comes
From God to pay our ransom and set us free,
Descending into the rank legion's home,
Taking on the cheek our violence,
Handing over to us his innocence.

John 18:13–14; Isaiah 53:11; Romans 5:12–17

311

PETER'S DENIAL

Peter and another followed from a distance.
His friend who knew Annas went inside,
Getting a servant girl to give them entrance,
The cold and fear making them want to hide.
As Peter was coming in—he was still armed—
She asked, "Are you with Jesus?" "I am not!"
Peter brushed her off and went to get warm.
Two more times he denied his God,
And then he heard the rooster crow again,
Plunging Peter into tears of woe,
Proving the prophecy of his dearest friend,
Who met his glance with sorrow. By this, he shows
There's nothing we can do to save our Lord,
But our denials grieve him, as do our swords.

Luke 22:54–62; John 18:15–18; Acts 3:13–14

312

PETER'S REMORSE

Every morning after that when the cock crew,
Peter wept bitterly. It tolled like a bell,
Each time he heard its cock-a-doodle-doo.
Grieving that he had played the infidel,
He began each day crying for mercy to God.
It kept him humble to think he had denied
His master three times before that awful dawn.
First to a maiden, a small white lie,
Second, more vehement, with an oath,
The third time, cursing with rage against his Lord,
And then the cock crew. Running outside, loath
To be seen publicly weeping in remorse,
The rock of the church split open by grief,
His sins ever before him in high relief.

Matthew 26:69–75; Judges 12:6; Psalm 51:3–4

313

THE SANHEDRIN'S QUESTIONING OF JESUS

They led Jesus, the way, the truth, the life,
Into Caiaphas, the reigning high priest,
Where they questioned him, the elders and scribes,
To make charges against him. He could not be released
Into the crowds again; he posed a threat.
They wanted false witnesses to testify
Against him, needing to put him to death.
Two gave evidence but did not lie
Saying he would tear the temple down
And build it up again in three days.
Caiaphas rose up, his robes swirling around,
Demanding Jesus answer him and say
He was the Christ, the Son of the living God,
Hoping for blasphemy, but it was not.

Matthew 26:59–63; Leviticus 5:1; Isaiah 53:7

314

CAIAPHAS QUESTIONS JESUS

Caiaphas pressed Jesus to blaspheme,
To say he was the Son of God. Jesus' retort
Stretched far beyond what Caiaphas had dreamed.
"You will witness the Son of Man," said our Lord,
"At the right hand of Power coming in the clouds
From heaven." Enough! The high priest tearing his robes
Asked those present, "What is your judgment now?"
"Death!" they cried, as Caiaphas had hoped.
The onlookers spit on Christ, striking his face,
Taunting him because he would not prophesy
And name who struck him. Suffering this disgrace,
Submitting to their abuse as they passed by,
Innocent that he had long ago foretold,
All the indignities that here unfold.

Matthew 26:63–66; Numbers 14:6–7; Hebrews 1:3

315

CHRIST BEFORE PILATE

Early the Day of Preparation they brought
Jesus, the Lamb of God, to Pilate's place,
The governor slept that night, but Christ did not.
Bound and dragged from the high priest's, slapped in the face,
He saw in the hours ahead the depths of hell.
Pilate came out to question our weary Lord:
What were the charges? He did not know himself.
Eager to return to their Passover chores,
They wanted Pilate to do their work for them,
Condemn our Lord for what he did not know,
Riling up the crowds in Jerusalem,
Urging the ruler representing Rome
To sacrifice for them this innocent
Stripped of his kingly mien, drained and spent.

John 18:28–32; Acts 10:28; 1 Timothy 6:13–16

316

JUDAS DESPAIRS

As morning broke over the sordid scene,
Judas watched them persecute his friend.
Guilt rushed over him, letting his laments keen
Into the courtyard, seeing where this would end.
The pieces of silver in his purse were a brood
Of condemnations. He went back to the priests
Crying, "I have sinned, betraying innocent blood!"
"What is that to us?" They gave no relief.
Tossing the silver coins on the temple floor,
Hearing them clatter on the marble as they fell,
Judas fled out of the open door.
Darkness overcame him; he hanged himself.
Finding his heart absent a spring of grace,
Only a slough of despond he could not face.

Matthew 27:3–5; 2 Samuel 17:23; Psalm 51:17

317

THE POTTER'S FIELD

They knew the silver thrown on the floor was blood
Money and could not be used for their own yield.
Thirty pieces of silver was enough,
The prophet said, to buy a potter's field
To bury strangers, the place where I belong,
Nailed to the cross, my rightful place, you gave
A field of blood, a ransom for my wrong,
To go before me to my beggar's grave.
You'll tell the driver of the hearse I'm in
That you have shouldered all the costs for me,
Paying the price for all my grievous sins
Coming to empty my tomb and set me free;
From death's last sentence, you will raise me up,
A potsherd ground to shape a brimming cup.

Matthew 27:6–10; Exodus 21:32; Zechariah 11:13

318

MY KINGDOM IS NOT OF THIS WORLD

Into the offices of Pilate he stepped,
Entering the world of empires and decrees;
All the stately marbles the governor kept
Showed his small province for everyone to see.
But Jesus reigned as king of something else,
Something the Roman prefect could not touch
With all his armored legions, truth itself.
It stopped the governor but not by much.
If Jesus had a kingdom, he must be king,
A threat to Caesar he could not understand
Nor fathom how his captive's words took wing;
All the invisible worlds at his command.
"What is truth?" he asks the truth, our Lord,
But does not stay to hear another word.

John 18:33–38; Daniel 2:44; 1 John 2:15–17

319

THE THREE CHARGES

They made their accusations against the Lord.
One, that he preached false doctrine to the crowds,
Then against taxes they could not afford,
And third, a king. This Pilate could not allow,
Asking Jesus, "Are you the King of the Jews?"
The Savior, regal, did not answer him,
Still not enough for Pilate to accuse
Jesus of insurrection. Out on a limb,
Pilate returned to say, "I find no guilt
In this man." The priests protested, "He stirs
Unrest in the people." The city filled
With pilgrims ready to act on rumors they heard
Scared him. Since Jesus came from Galilee,
He sent him to Herod, hoping they'd both be freed.

Luke 23:4–7; Acts 4:26; 1 Peter 2:21–25

320

HEROD AND THE GORGEOUS ROBE

Herod longed to meet this rival king,
Himself aspiring to be King of the Jews,
Hoping Jesus would do magic things
While he pranced around him. Jesus stood
Silently. Herod had blood on his hands,
Beheading John the Baptist for a girl
Whose salacious dancing undid the man.
His lust drove him to kill in a wanton whirl.
Now laughing in this play of dreadful parts,
Dressing the Lord in scarlet robes for fun,
Mocking the prince before him, his dauntless heart,
Jeering and sneering at God's only Son.
The ironies of this parody are cruel:
He craved Christ's title but only proved the fool.

Luke 23:6–12; Psalm 2:2; Acts 4:27–28

321

BARABBAS AND PILATE'S WIFE

With Pilate again, our Lord would only speak
When the prefect asked, "Are you the King of the Jews?"
"You have said so," his body growing weak
After hours of questioning. Then Jesus refused
To answer anything. The governor thought
To offer Jesus for Barabbas, the crowds
Could decide. Out to the mob, Pilate brought
The murderer Barabbas, bloody, unbowed.
Pilate's wife, watching all his schemes
And troubled by the unrest in the court,
Wrote what she had suffered in a dream.
"Have nothing to do with him," she told her lord.
Legend has it she heard millions say his name
In a creed confessing his perfidy and shame.

Matthew 27:15–23; Mark 15:11; Acts 13:28

322

JESUS SCOURGED

Barabbas to be freed, Jesus scourged.
Here in a sentence read the gospel truth.
The guilty saved, and Jesus bears the curse
We should have borne, saving us from the sharp tooth
Of the Law, needing to bite for justice to be done.
But the mobs demand Barabbas be set free
And Jesus die, the Father's innocent Son.
God uses their evil for good so I can be
Given the life he loses for my sake,
Even as I egg on the men with their whips
Against my God. Nary a sound he makes;
No complaints or sorrows cross his lips.
He looks at me, knowing he will swallow up
All of the darkness filling his bitter cup.

Mark 15:6–15; Isaiah 53:3–9; Acts 3:14–15

323

MOCKERY OF JESUS

Dressed in the regal purples, a gorgeous frock,
He stood up from his scourging. They wove a crown
Of thorns to press on his head, a scepter to mock
His royal claims. Spitting and kneeling down,
The Roman battalion who had come to despise
Their Jewish subjects tried to make a fool
Of our Lord, ridiculing his disguise,
Crying out, "Hail! O King of the Jews!"
Their scoffing has not ended. Many grieve
Our Lord, taunting those who follow him,
Laughing at Christians who say they still believe.
They jeer at him, thinking his light has dimmed.
Here stands the Light of the World, our King, his grace,
Blood dripping with tears down his regal face.

John 19:2–3; Matthew 27:27–30; Psalm 69:19–21

324

BEHOLD! THE MAN

Bloody from the lashing and the crown of thorns,
Jesus in his purple cloak stumbles out
With Pilate from the palace; hurt, forlorn,
He stands silent hearing Pilate shout,
"I have found no guilt in him. Behold! the man!"
Pointing at Jesus, the Son of God made flesh,
Whom we are drawn to, but reason cannot stand.
It scandalizes us to need this death.
To behold him is to see our sin made clear.
Stricken, smitten, and afflicted, the Christ,
Whose stripes will heal us, must die to bring us near,
The Passover Lamb who will be sacrificed.
"Crucify! Crucify!" We want him dead,
Our scapegoat dressed for slaughter drawn and bled.

John 19:4–7; Leviticus 24:16; Isaiah 52:13–14

325

SON OF GOD

Now Pilate had grown even more afraid
Hearing that Jesus might be a god's son.
His Roman pieties came into play.
He knew the stories of what the gods had done
Consorting with humans. Aeneas, founder of Rome,
Son of Aphrodite, goddess of love,
And Anchises, a prince of Troy, carried from his home
By his son. Was this man Jesus, born from above,
The stuff of legends? Did Pilate catch a glimpse
Of another world breaking into his own?
Pedestrian, worried, feeling himself a wimp.
Frightened, he pondered, pacing the ancient stones,
Why Jesus had powers that he had not been given.
Could it be this man had come from heaven?

John 19:7–9; Isaiah 53:7; 1 Peter 2:23–24

326

CHRIST STANDS BEFORE PILATE AGAIN

The truth stands before him, bloody, bruised,
A twisted crown of thorns upon his head,
As Pilate questions him. "Just who are you?
A king? Of what? They're plotting your death."
A judge, he could not issue his decree.
His craven spirit wavered, troubling him.
Jesus was not guilty; he should set him free.
To keep the rabble in Jerusalem
Under control, he had to do their will.
He saw the majesty in Jesus' face.
Beside him all his earthly powers failed.
He felt his bones melting, his body waste,
His very being false: behold the man
Washing the truth from his guilty hands.

Matthew 27:24–25; Psalm 73:14; Isaiah 53:8–9

327

BEHOLD! YOUR KING

High noon, the Passover lambs are being killed.
Pilate leads Jesus out to the judgment seat,
Saying, "Behold your king!" He cannot yield,
The threat to Caesar could bring his own defeat,
Ousted by Rome and bereft of his small powers,
Tiberius would not suffer a competing force;
Christ must be crucified; now is the hour!
The mobs shout, "Crucify!" Their earthly lord
And king is Caesar. Blasphemy now their cry.
The morning sun beating on the pavement stones
Blinds their sight, echoing, "Crucify!"
His fate in the balance, Pilate acts alone
And hands over the sacrificial Lamb
On the mount where Isaac climbed with Abraham.

John 19:12–16; Genesis 22:1–19; Revelation 5:12

328

BLOOD CURSE

Oh, the regrets Christians should have around
This passage. It has caused oceans of blood
To be shed in the killing fields of cursed ground.
Believers must repent of the awful flood
Of persecutions this dreadful sentence caused,
Finding warrants in the terrible line
For private shunning; church and national laws
Causing holocausts of Jewish lives.
I am the guilty one, drowning in guilt.
Standing there watching with the unruly mob
Crying to heaven that innocent blood be spilled,
Outraged by this fool claiming to be God,
Unmoved by the shame pouring into his cup,
Calling for blood to cover my treachery up.

Matthew 27:24–25; Numbers 35:33; Isaiah 50:6

329

PILATE RELEASES BARABBAS

Three times Pilate declared Christ innocent,
Wishing he could release him. The mob cried,
"Free Barabbas!" An insurrectionist
And murderer. For this, he should have died,
But Pilate freed him, making evil good:
We are all Barabbas, bound by sin,
Whom reason would keep chained, a dark brood
Sunk into terror. Then a torch begins
To flicker outside our cell. The iron clanks,
And, blinking in the morning sun, we see
Another carrying our cross. How can we thank
This one we crucified who sets us free?
Joyful, we kneel down on the pavement stones
Amazed by the grace in our stiffened, guilty bones.

Luke 23:22–25; Proverbs 17:15; Romans 5:6–11

330

CARRYING THE CROSS

The sentence given, Pilate can go home,
As Jesus staggers under the weight of the cross.
Mobs taunting him, the soldiers working for Rome
Are doing their duty and do not mark the loss.
Weakened by his beatings, Jesus needs help.
Simon of Cyrene standing in the crowd
Is drafted. Taking Christ's burden on himself,
He sees the stripes on his back and his bloody brow.
On their way, darkness begins to shadow the sun
As though it cannot bear to see the sight
Of Golgotha, where these grisly deeds are done.
Outside the city gate, the world's true light
Will be lifted up as pious people scoff,
Stripping his last piece of clothing off.

Matthew 27:32–33; Numbers 15:35; Hebrews 13:12–14

331

DAUGHTERS OF JERUSALEM

The women of Jerusalem had cried,
"Hosanna! Crucify!" and now lament
His suffering, seeing him on his way to die,
Weeping for his wounds, filled with kind sentiments.
But Jesus pushes back on their well-meant tears.
He does not need their sympathy; look ahead,
He says, "Weep for your own fate. See it near.
The day will come when you will wish you were dead,
Praying that mountains would fall on you and kill
Both you and your children. Your pity will not do
Anything to stop my dying. It is my will.
I have been sent to take away your sins for you,
To give you life. Look into your heart.
See in its darkness the world falling apart."

Luke 23:27–31; Hosea 10:8; Revelation 6:16

332

THE GREEN TREE AND THE DRY

New cut wood that is green does not burn
Easily unless a conflagration ignites
The fresh leaves and wet wood. It rarely turns
The living vine to ash, but a dry branch lights
Up with only a small spark, and it starts
Raging fires. Jesus is the green tree,
Fresh as Eden, young and new at heart,
Heavy with moisture, brimming with life for me.
But look, we cut him down, our branches dry,
The slightest embers exploding into flame;
Thus we will perish of our deadness, die
From the fury our rotten branches cannot tame.
A bonfire of vanities, my funeral pyre,
Only the living water can quench this fire.

Luke 23:31; Proverbs 11:31; Ezekiel 20:47–49

333

THE CRUCIFIXION

When they reached Golgotha, the place of the skull,
They crucified him. Shaming him, stripping him nude,
Pounding into his wrists the lethal nails,
His body lying flat against the wood.
Staring up into the heavens, unnaturally dark,
His arms stretch out as if to draw the earth
And all its denizens into his arms.
Lifted up, the great I AM from his birth.
Here in the shuddering settling of the brute cross
Into the ground, a strange glory appears.
In this moment, the flesh sees only loss,
But faith beholds the living God come near
To take away our sin so we can live
In the new world our king is dying to give.

John 19:16–18; Jeremiah 23:5; 1 Corinthians 1:28–30

334

FATHER, FORGIVE THEM

The Lord's Prayer from the cross, his first word:
"Father, forgive them; they know not what they do,"
The din of hammers, jeering, screeching birds,
Omens of evil, as the darkness grew,
Ravens circling the dying men for meat,
Mobs wagging their heads, scoffing at their king.
Naked and thirsty, losing his body heat,
He looks down toward the crowd—his salt tears sting—
Seeing sinners he is dying to forgive,
Bored onlookers, listless soldiers, priests and friends,
The wise and simple, he came for us to live,
Though we rarely give a thought to our final ends.
Rubbing our fingers against a broken nail,
We shrug off his absolution. A grave detail.

Luke 23:34; Isaiah 53:12; Romans 12:14

335

THE KING OF THE JEWS

He meant it in derision but told the truth.
The first Gospel, one that Pilate wrote,
Over the head of Jesus, "King of the Jews,"
A title all the temple leaders loathed.
"Change it," they demanded, "so it can be read
'He said, I am the King of the Jews.'" "Away,"
Pilate commanded with a surge of strength.
"What I have written I have written! It stays."
Three tongues telling the nations about this man.
A king sent to all the world from here,
From the chosen people, where the lineage began.
Jesus, the Son of David, making clear
From Calvary we can trace the royal line
Back to the house of David: read the sign.

John 19:19–22; Esther 4:16; Daniel 7:14

336

CASTING LOTS FOR HIS GARMENTS

Stripped naked of his garments, in utter shame,
Soldiers under him gamble for his clothes,
A seamless garment the spoils of their game.
Beneath the cross, irreverent, none of them knows
This is the hour the drama will be done.
Mary wove the robe without a seam,
Now desecrated before her dying Son
As they toss the dice. Hanging between
Heaven and the looming pit of hell
The Lord of all creation. We always miss
The main event; the soldiers cannot tell
Its elemental depths, a yawning abyss,
The fabric of horror. Our God is dying; they play
A game of chance for all the day's remains.

John 19:23–24; Matthew 27:35–36; Psalm 22:18

337

BEHOLD YOUR SON;
BEHOLD YOUR MOTHER

Mary, his mother, at the foot of the cross in tears
With the beloved disciple at her side,
Weeping as old Simeon's sword pierced
Her heart, her righteous Son now crucified.
Bewildered by the cruel events that day,
Whose crumbs could she scavenge, a widow and poor?
Christ read her terror, looking down to say,
"Woman, behold your Son!" He opened a door:
"Behold your Mother," he instructed John
Who took her home with him. Kin without blood,
Relatives born of water, mother and son,
Jesus forming a church in baptism's flood,
A congregation engendered by his word,
Knit together in a fold of what they heard.

John 19:25–27; Luke 2:34–35; Galatians 3:25–29

338

MOCKERY OF JESUS ON THE CROSS

Wagging their heads, it is the truth they mock.
They do not understand the words they say
Are pure gospel. He did not leave his cross
To save himself; he would not disobey.
"He came to save others, not himself,"
Scoffing at the truth, the mystery of Christ.
He died for us, we would have nothing else
But pain needling us to death. His sacrifice
Ends what is old. Like the tempter long ago,
We want him to abandon the love he brought
And fall to earth, to realities we know.
Our words mock him; we miss the truth: Son of God.
"He trusts in God" to raise him from the tomb
In three days, failing to see his temple loom.

Matthew 27:39–44; Psalm 22:7–8; Hebrews 10:33

339

ONE THIEF MOCKS JESUS

One of the thieves joined the mocking priests,
Desperate for rescue. "If you are the Christ,
Save yourself and us." He wanted release,
A thief trying to make his final heist
Railing at Jesus for not being God.
The other, taking his punishment, confessed
His sin, his life of thievery and fraud.
In the darkness, he wanted to be blessed.
Dying to his flesh and sin, he needed grace.
Through the ruins of the day, he glimpsed
The kingdom where Christ rules, a better place.
Despite his agony and tortured limbs,
He asks the Prince of Glory, weak and faint,
To be remembered in his coming reign.

Luke 23:39–43; Romans 6:5–11; 1 Timothy 6:13–16

340

THE THIRD WORD FROM THE CROSS

A royal clemency, we hear it ring:
"Today you shall be with me in paradise!"
Words from the cross from a reigning king
Sound through the universe before he dies.
Soon, he will ascend to the heavenly courts,
Take up his scepter, and greet the shriven thief.
We caused this death, so Jesus is made Lord
In an alchemy of joy and grief.
The sun, the moon, and stars at his command
Maintain their courses; in heaven, the gates of pearl
Open with choruses of angels at his right hand.
Eden is restored, the garden of the world.
He came to grant his subjects paradise.
In him, the old world meets its end and dies.

Luke 23:43; 2 Corinthians 12:3–4; Revelation 2:7

341

MY GOD, MY GOD, WHY HAVE YOU FORSAKEN ME?

Darkness, thick darkness, over all the land
As Jesus takes on sin for all of us.
God's holiness shrinks away; it cannot stand
Sin's incarnation hanging on the cross.
Jesus cries out, "My God, my God," for help.
"My God! Why have you forsaken me?"
A cry of dereliction, his descent to hell,
Taking into his flesh our treachery.
Jesus will perish utterly alone
As he takes our sin into himself. His last breath,
Bringing an end to these failures all our own,
Our sin crucified with him in his death
To bury on the shelves of his borrowed tomb
All the grave endings that spell our doom.

Matthew 27:45–49; Psalm 22:1–2; 2 Corinthians 5:21

342

I THIRST!

The living water, dying, says, "I thirst!"
Like Moses once, he could have struck a rock
And waited for the springs of water to burst
From stone. He does no magic nor overlooks
Nature's seasons to relieve his pain.
All flesh is grass, and he is truly flesh,
Thirsty as the flower of the field needing rain.
The seed needs water as it meets its death.
They give him sour wine to moisten his lips.
The hyssop passes over him; he tastes
His ending in the portion that he sips.
Looking down at the mob, the foes he faced,
He drinks to the lees transgressions in his cup,
Watering the death he needs to be raised up.

John 19:28; Exodus 12:22; Hebrews 10:11–14

343

IT IS FINISHED

"It is finished!" he cries and sips the wine,
Then bows his head as the ravens swoop and croak
Smelling the taste of death. Their battle lines
In disarray, Satan's forces break
Rank and scatter, his slimy head bruised
By Christ's wounded heel, Eden's prophecy
Come true. His death the death of death. Good news.
The mourners standing below him hardly see
The triumph here. He will be raised and never die
Again. His crucifixion lifting the curse,
Unraveling the tangles in Satan's lies,
Restoring us to an unsullied universe.
Redeemed by the bloody sacrifice we craved,
Contrary to our wishes, a deed that saves.

John 19:30; Genesis 3:15; Isaiah 55:10–11

344

INTO YOUR HANDS, FATHER, I COMMEND MY SPIRIT

Bowing his head, Jesus handed over
His Spirit to his Father. A faithful Son
Obedient unto death, his calm composure
Trusting in God to raise him, the victory won.
All of nature stops, stunned by the scene,
Gasping for breath, filling all flesh with dread.
The priests go home for dinner; the women keen
Over his body stiffening with pale death.
We wanted to shut him up, to keep the peace.
Now that he has breathed his last, the shock
And horror stop us, we see his breath cease,
Its consequence begins to dawn, we balk
At our complicity; his body cold,
His mother, weeping, cannot be consoled.

Luke 23:46; Psalm 31:5; Acts 7:59–60

345

HE BREATHED HIS LAST

He breathed his last; now with a loud cry, his breath
Went out of him, back into Adam's dust
Before God filled his nostrils with air and death
Darkened the first couple's simple trust.
A cosmic ending here outside the gate,
We felt the stays of the universe contract
To see its God crucified by hate.
All that is holy desecrated by our acts.
Nothing we do can have our sins dispelled.
The Lamb of God has died to take our sins,
Bury them in his grave, the pit of hell,
So like the freshest Eden, life can begin
Anew. To live again, we first must die
To all the sin dreading this final cry.

John 19:30; 1 Thessalonians 5:9–11; Philippians 2:8–10

346

THE DEATH OF JESUS

Christ's death rattles the bedrock of the earth
And heaven, shaking things up. The curtain torn
In the holy of holies, the temple's rebirth
As Jesus goes to raze it. For this, he was born:
To break God out of the ancient ark,
Making familiar everything divine;
Shattering the basalt rocks, rifts in the dark,
Emptying scattered graves, a godly sign
To show God's power. And as the mountain quakes,
The soldiers chorus, "Truly, the Son of God!"
The ground rumbling under them, they feel truth break,
Confessing Jesus in the words the priests had mocked.
The women, Christ's ministers, looking on,
Weep, trying to fathom the death of God's own Son.

Matthew 27:51–56; Exodus 26:31–35; Hebrews 9:6–10

347

THE SWORD PIERCING JESUS' SIDE

Adam gave birth to Eve from his rib, his side.
Noah walked into a new world from the side of the ark.
Now a soldier, after Christ has died,
Pierces Christ's mortal body, on a lark,
Stunned to witness rushing water and blood
Pouring from his side, proving him human flesh,
Feeding the infant church in its flood.
John and Mary ponder his awful death,
Remembering the ancient prophecy
Of God being pierced in the side with a spear.
Weeping bitterly for all this cruelty,
All of creation joining with their tears,
Water and blood gushing—see his corpse lurch.
He gives birth to a bride waiting to be churched.

John 19:30; Zechariah 12:10–11; Hebrews 9:22

348

THE WOMEN MINISTERS

The women who loved him watched from some distance off.
They had followed him from Galilee,
Some ninety miles, caring for him, for love.
His special sense for them had set them free.
He gave them the courage to go against the rules
And wait beneath the cross. His disciples had fled
Into the city, leaving him, like fools
Panicked to think their Master would be dead.
Mary Magdalene, in her tear-soaked hair,
Chief of the mourners, knew what her Lord had done,
Giving her health, saving her from despair.
Heavy with grief, weeping for Adam's son,
She stands her ground, daring what most would not,
Braving the rabble of the devil's plot.

Matthew 27:55–56; Psalm 38:11; Luke 8:1–3

349

JESUS' BURIAL

Jesus' corpse had to be taken from the cross
Before the Sabbath to keep the ancient rules.
This was Passover; they knew the laws.
Joseph of Arimathea, a faithful Jew,
Loved the Lord. He went to Pilate, asked him
For leave to bury the body in his tomb
Next to Calvary, outside Jerusalem,
In a garden, like Eden, as evening loomed.
Nicodemus, who had not quite believed,
Now confessed his faith with sacks of myrrh.
They took the body down, wrapped it while they grieved,
Planted it in the tomb with a stone to deter
Vultures from breaking in to desecrate
The body. Outside, the faithful women wait.

John 19:38–42; Genesis 2:8–9; 2 Chronicles 16:14

350

THE GUARDS AT THE TOMB

Fearing they would steal the body of their Lord,
The chief priests wanted to stop his followers' lies
That might claim his resurrection, the word
They feared, beyond belief that he would rise.
Asking Pilate to set a guard to watch,
They sealed the stone and waited. Before dawn
The third day, they felt a lightning bolt flash,
An angel descend, rolling back the stone.
The guards trembled and lay like men who were dead.
The body in the grave had disappeared.
Was it alive? The frightened soldiers fled
To tell the chief priests news they would not hear.
They paid the soldiers to lie and never tell
The truth they spent their days trying to spell.

Matthew 27:62–66; Matthew 28:11–15; Revelation 1:17–18

351

THE WOMEN AT THE TOMB

Up early, before dawn, the women, weary with grief,
Gathered their spices, preparing to lave the corpse
To stave off the odors of death and find relief
In the ministries of love for their martyred Lord.
The night before, they'd watched the stone being rolled
Against the entrance of the tomb and feared
Nothing could move it away, nothing could hold
Back the worm of death. Then earth shook; they heard
Angels descending like lightning, Eden's cherubim, dawn broke
"Be not afraid! You seek Jesus, the crucified.
He is not here; he is risen!" Dawn broke in them.
Frightened and joyful, the women peered inside,
Nothing but folded clothes where he had lain.
They ran out into a new world now right as rain.

Matthew 28:1–10; Daniel 10:6; Revelation 18:1

352

JOHN AND PETER RUN TO THE GRAVE

Mary ran to tell Peter and John
The stone had been rolled away from the tomb.
When they heard, they ran, wondering where he had gone.
The younger man ran faster and looked in the room
Seeing the cloths. Peter went in first
And saw the folded cloth for Jesus' head.
Had he been taken by an enemy, still accursed?
But John quickly believed what Scripture said,
That on the third day he would rise. Peter, slow
To understand what both of them had seen,
Led the way home. Their reason could not know
The miracle, but Mary Magdalene
Stayed behind, wanting to be near,
A small grain in her knowing he would appear.

John 20:1–4; Isaiah 26:9; Proverbs 8:17

353

DO NOT HOLD ME

A wilderness of sorrow in the stone,
She stands in the garden like our mother Eve
Cast out, in exile, left behind, alone.
All she can do, gazing at the rock, is grieve.
"Where have you put him, sir?" The grave is wide.
Robbed of her one last time to touch his flesh,
Clasping his corpse to her, like a widowed bride.
Inside the marble shelf, odors of death;
All he had said perishing in his tomb.
Dropping to the ground, she heard the voice
Deep as creation, fresh as a flower, bloom.
A move, a sound she fathoms, the depths rejoice.
Love that has risen out of death will hold
These cultivations in a flight of gold.

John 20:11–18; Song of Songs 2:8; 1 Peter 1:3–5

354

APOSTLE TO THE APOSTLES

"Mariam!" Jesus calls her by her name.
Suddenly wrenched from grief and certain death
To joy, the first to see Eden reclaimed:
A man raised from the dead! It takes her breath
Away, an unknown heaven in her arms
Pointing her to wonders that have no end.
A new dimension touches her tear-soaked garb,
Embracing a god who came to be her friend,
All of her longing satisfied for good.
He sent her off to tell them the good news
Healing the rift. Eve would have understood.
Mary had seen the new Adam bruise
The tempter's head. His death the end of the world
She knows. She feels the ground move, the heavens whirl.

John 20:11–18; Genesis 3:8–20; Ephesians 1:15–21

355

CHRIST APPEARS TO PETER
AFTER THE RESURRECTION

Before he walked the long Emmaus road,
Jesus met Peter. There's not much that we hear
Describing it. Peter's heavy load
Of guilt for his denials, his righteous fear
That Jesus would reject him, must have filled
His heart with terror. What would Jesus say?
He had seen the empty tomb by Calvary's hill.
Later in the early hours of the third day,
He saw the Lord shining before him. Did he drop
To the ground, tears gushing at the sight
Of his resurrected Lord? Did his wonder stop
His chatter? To see, standing in waves of light,
The full shape of Jesus risen from the dead
Turned him toward wonder from every tear he'd shed.

Luke 24:34; Acts 10:39–42; 1 Corinthians 15:5

356

ON THE ROAD TO EMMAUS

Baffled and brokenhearted, they left for home,
To Emmaus, rehearsing the events
Of the past week. A presence they did not know
Joined their conversation as they went
Along the way. "What are you talking about?"
He asked. Their answer would become a creed
Stating the facts they knew. They did not doubt
The reports they heard but had no faith to believe.
"O foolish ones and slow of heart," he cried,
"The prophets have spoken; it should all be clear!"
He opened up Scripture, why he had to die
Beginning with Moses. They listened but did not hear.
Their wisdom could only see folly in this loss
As they stumbled over the glory of his cross.

Luke 24:13–27; Micah 7:16–20; 1 Corinthians 1:18–25

357

DID NOT OUR HEARTS
BURN WITHIN US?

"Abide with us, for it is evening, the day
Is far spent." Without knowing it,
They craved his light, asking him to stay
And break bread with them. The candles lit,
He took the new baked loaf, the meal began.
Blessing it, he gave it to them. In a flash of light,
Gold blossomed in his nail-scarred hands.
Later, they marveled as they ran through the night:
His word opened their eyes; they could see
Immanuel unveiled, radiant and true,
The dead raised up, Moses and the prophecies
Pointing to the resurrection, old flesh made new.
Their hearts in flames on their hurried walk,
Faith winging toward them in his burning talk.

Luke 24:28–35; Psalm 39:3–4; Jeremiah 33:14–16

358

RESURRECTED JESUS
APPEARS TO APOSTLES

His resurrected body suddenly appeared
Through locked doors standing in their midst.
In him, the earth and heavens are brought near.
His gestures still the same, the voice was his,
The nail prints in his hands, his pierced side.
He blessed them with a benediction, "Peace!"
They knew eternity in flesh that night.
He set their spirits rising as he breathed
Into their hearts his Spirit's life and gave
All of them wondering in that quiet room
A new world, one they soon would have to brave
As he sent them forward from the empty tomb
To preach forgiveness, that death had met defeat,
The truth to tell from his wounded hands and feet.

John 20:19–23; Isaiah 60:1–3; 2 Timothy 2:1–3

359

DOUBTING THOMAS

We praise Thomas for his vocal doubt,
For his need to see the Savior's nail-pierced hands
And put his fingers there to find them out,
Placing his hands in his side, bold demands.
Eight days later, Christ appeared in the room,
Giving them peace after passing through locked doors,
Bringing light to Thomas's faithless gloom.
He told him to put his hand in his sores.
And believe. Seeing, Thomas's doubt fled.
"My Lord and my God!" He told the truth
Without a shred of doubt. Jesus looked ahead
Toward us and spoke a new beatitude,
"Blessed are those who have not seen but believe."
Faith does not come from proofs a body sees.

John 20:24–29; 1 Peter 1:6–9; 1 John 3:2

360

CATCH OF 153 FISH

Sitting in the boat without a single bite,
Dawn broke; a voice cried, "Have you any fish?"
Peering at the sun they could not see for light.
The voice commanded, and then without a hitch,
The nets filled with a silver roiling; they knew
The Lord was stoking the fire, ready to grill
Their catch on the beach. Out of the blue,
A god cooking their breakfast, eating his fill,
Tasting the fish that had not got away.
New realms break through. Jesus prophesies
They're like the old man who cannot find his way
But fathoms all that faith cannot deny.
He'll lead them to places they do not want to go,
Beyond the light and what they do not know.

John 21:1–14; Psalm 126:6; Isaiah 20:2

361

SIMON, SON Of JOHN, DO YOU LOVE ME?

Jesus asks after breakfast on the beach
If Peter loves him more than all the rest.
Peter answers with a kind of pique,
"You know I love you!" Is this some kind of test?
Jesus answers, "Feed my lambs!" Now two,
"Simon, son of John, do you love me?"
Peter explodes, "Lord, you know I do!"
The Lord replies, "Then, Simon, tend my sheep!"
And then a third time, "Simon, do you love
Me?" grieving Peter to hear it yet again.
Once, he thought, would have been enough.
"Feed my sheep!" Jesus tells his friend,
Making each confession wipe away
The stain of his three denials that awful day.

John 21:15–19; 1 Chronicles 28:9; Hebrews 13:20–21

362

PETER ASKS ABOUT JOHN

Peter wonders about the place of John—
A titch of jealousy, maybe, appears.
John, the beloved, will be staying on
With Jesus; Peter will lead. Christ is clear:
"You follow me!" he hears his Lord command,
"Do what you do best. Soon, I will send you forth
Into all the world. Forget about this man!"
He will abide; Peter travel the earth.
John, caring for Mary, will stay to write,
Telling the Gospel that will bring us to belief;
Like an eagle, he will see the story from the heights,
Handing over the truths the church must receive
As a firsthand witness to eternal things
At the foot of the cross where Christ became our king.

John 21:20–24; Hebrews 10:37–38; Revelation 2:25

363

THE GREAT COMMISSION

Well met in Galilee, where he began
His ministry now spreading over the earth.
They wait for him on the mountain, as he had planned,
To hear from his mouth his final words.
Even now in their worship, some still doubt.
It shadows them when they gather on the hill
As the vision of Daniel brightens and comes about:
He takes all his authority when he tells
The eleven to go forth into all the world,
Making disciples of all the nations,
Baptizing and teaching all the truths that whirl
Out of his commands through all creation.
"Be fruitful, and multiply the seeds I've sown.
Harvest and plant them, nourish them, make me known."

Matthew 28:16–20; Genesis 1:28; Romans 1:1–6

364

JESUS APPEARS TO JAMES, THE
FIVE HUNDRED, AND PAUL

They had to see it to speak of the unseen:
A resurrected body, pure light and grace.
Jesus revealing all he had redeemed,
A new dimension fluttering through our space
At the same time showing what flesh could never know
Until its end pouring over into light.
We try to dream of places we cannot go,
Building them with measures no one can write.
Jesus must come to us to show his hands,
Confirming the winged nature of our calls
Sealed in bright words we barely understand,
Knowing a wonder waits down a narrow hall,
All we imagine not enough to prove
What we behold, a body of pure love.

1 Corinthians 15:5–8; Luke 24:34; Acts 9:1–9

365

THE ASCENSION Of JESUS

Still looking for the type of king they knew,
One like King David, in a palace to reign
Justly and make Israel, out of the blue,
A great empire, restore his kingdom again,
The disciples gather one last time to see
Jesus and contemplate what kind of king
He is: the ruler of eternity,
Who came into our troubled world to bring
All of the wealth his Father has to give
To woo his bride. The glory of the heavens,
Our bridegroom, come to us so we might live
Free from the bondage to ourselves forever.
Into his Father's mansions, he disappears,
Sending his Spirit, the power to keep him near.

Acts 1:6–9; Deuteronomy 29:29; Revelation 22:17–21

366

THESE WERE WRITTEN SO YOU MIGHT BELIEVE IN JESUS

Not all the books in all the world can contain
Christ's beauty, his miracles, the way he lived.
His Spirit hovers over us; he reigns
King of a realm whose glories are kept hid
Until faith opens our eyes and we see
Jesus standing before us like the sun,
Himself the temple where earth and heaven meet,
The tree of paradise blooming in us,
And the constellation around which all things whirl
In orbs of light. Their radiants sing for joy
As all creation, spinning world on world,
Hymns the praise of Jesus, a baby boy
Born in a stable, suffering, crucified,
Crowned now by stars, the home where we abide.

John 20:30–31; John 21:25; Colossians 1:15–20